What is Society?

*

essay

*

Traumear

A critique of society as environment

There is the society that prepares us for community, but there is also the society that rejects community. In this essay we hope to make the difference more clear in terms of how we behave while we fear for our individuality when we might rise to the occasion of human-natural affinity. The emphasis is placed on our willingness to familiarize ourselves gradually more and more with the content of our desire for communal love in the face of a corporality based on fear. – I dedicate this book to those who are rejected by society and to those who have opted out of society, and finally to those who practice communal living based on their human-natural affinity and who therefore no longer have a quarrel with society. It is their struggle that is depicted in this book.

* * *

What is society?

1

The truth of the matter or else the unlimited extent of the subject beyond all bounds of reason and usefulness – this seems to be the choice – and also perhaps an explanation for that pervasive unwillingness to distinguish between social being and social doing along lines other than morality and expediency. While the sociologist assumes that something about society may be truly known, the mass media invite us to flirt with the notion of endless riches to be gained by un-questioning immersion in society as a thing in itself, as a state of being that finally and wholly satisfies. The search, some-times almost frantic, for the assurance of objectivity, is in-variably accompanied by a growing sense of alienation, whereupon the pendulum swings back to indulgence in the sentiment of belonging, to the fostering of a group psyche and the eventual insistence on institution to sustain it.

*

2

Upon some contemplation of it in essence, society reveals itself as what is happening, however what is happen-ing is viewed as though it were intentional and planned. Con-ventionally when we say that something is happening – or has happened, for that matter – we generally agree that at least for the moment (but perhaps for all time) it makes no sense to speak of a cause or of a causal agent. While we sup-pose that no one intended or planned it we are willing to de-scribe it as having happened. We ally the event of it, in our minds or expressly, with luck, with accident and chance, or we call it fate. It's a way of saying that we cannot possibly imagine how 'it' might have been caused. The tree falling in front of the speeding car does not cause the accident but if a

1

man pushed the tree over, he did cause it, either by malice aforethought or through neglect.

No one is responsible for what happens. No one *can* be responsible for it. It will help if right from the start we think of responsibility as first and foremost not a chore or a 'guilt-trip' but as an ability, indeed as the ability, to respond. I would wish gladly to be responsible for my actions and when I have behaved in a way that results in my hoping to be able to deny my responsibility for the effect of the behaviour, I have something to regret. On the other hand if something has happened and I pretend to be responsible for it, I am either indulging a morbid streak or sailing on borrowed wind.

My mental intention, my bodily disposition, a physical plan I have – all these are tributaries into a context of action for which I want to be responsible. My response is what I come up with when what I have done rebounds on me. When I rush in like a fool I am bowled over by the repercussions because I have acted or behaved 'irresponsibly'.

So whenever my activity or behaviour is mostly mental, or emphatically bodily, or a physical combination of the two, I do well to exercise at the same time my ability to respond to any consequences of what I am setting in train. I may think of the responsibility as in addition to the action and it does no harm to bring it in as early as the disposition or intention.

The only action that comes along with responsibility, so to speak, readily built into it, is creative or spiritual action, by way of my operant soul. A creative act cannot be intended. One cannot predispose oneself for it or plan it. By a creative act I mean one that originates in merciful good spirit. What I can do of course is exist in such a way that I will be more ready to behave or act creatively when the time to do so comes, but the time definitely has to come. By comparison, when I intend and dispose and plan, I do so in my own good time.

*

3

How does society happen? When two or three of us get together thoughtlessly? That may be it in a nutshell.

But what exactly is it that happens when two or three of us get together like that, intending nothing, not disposing ourselves in any way?

For the moment let's take the term 'society' on faith, as if we had never heard it before. If I myself, by myself, just drift along into the blue, neither alert nor attentive during the course of a perfectly good day, I build up trouble for myself, that goes without saying. The many influences to which every creature is always exposed, knowingly or unknowingly, do not meet a response in me and instead a pathological state comes about in me. The creative influence of reality on me does not meet with, or rather end in, my creative response but in my pathetic condition. I become ill or sick, in the broader sense. Now I have something more tangible to work with, if I choose, namely the pain I can suffer, but what a pity that I did not respond to the intangible influence of reality and save myself all that pain! A credible awareness of real spirit would have been a prerequisite, of course.

So I suppose one might say that the first adult thing for me to learn is that reality exists and that it exists creatively in my favour and that things eventually become painful for me if I ignore that. My responsive creativity ends in life for me but my ignorant inattentiveness and unreceptiveness ends in pain and death.

When two or three of us get together irresponsibly, not only is the pathetic conditioning in me stepped up but an element of catastrophe, of breakdown, comes into play. What is more, (or rather less) – it happens to be a pleasure. Not only is my integrity undermined but its demise is hastened. This is what happens. It has nothing yet to do with society, only with irresponsibility multiplied.

I may notice what is going on. I may notice the pleasure and I may notice something suspect about the pleasure. I may notice the shared self-satisfaction and the fact that it is happening. I may not do any more than notice this, in which case the disintegration proceeds unimpeded.

On the other hand I may draw some conclusions about what is happening. Above all I may end up making certain judgements. Very likely these will be judgements of one or two things that are being done, when in fact nothing is being done at all. This is a most peculiar state of affairs and a unique turn of events. Why am I making decisions like this? More to the point, why do I suppose that what merely happens is being done? Is this just a simple mistake or is there method to my madness?

For the answer to this question we have to reflect on the more basic situation at that time, the defining characteristic of which happens to be my lack of contact with reality and my sinking or sliding into a pleasurable state of unreality. Why do we not all just keep sliding until the coffin lid is nailed down? Why do I make decisions, albeit wrong ones?

It's because I have noticed in the past how this pleasure that accompanies our collectivity does not last but gives way to pain. I don't realize that the pleasure is not real but morbid, that the collectivity is not communality. I mistake both of them for the real thing. My ambition therefore is bound to be a prolongation of the pleasure and a prevention of the pain.

So much for the underlying, basic situation. Having been caught in an unreal state, and mindful of both present pleasure and future pain, I decide to be sociable, in the interest of prolonged pleasure and prevented pain.

How am I sociable? First of all by pretending that this prolongation and prevention is possible – which means that I am actually doing something now – and then by soliciting a similar pretension from those around me. The one type of behaviour, of sociability, really answers to both needs. I sense that my pleasure and the pleasure of those in the same unreal state with me are not to be separated. Let's all pretend that this situation is workable, that it is sustainable in such a way that the pleasure will outweigh the pain.

Part and parcel of this collective pretending now is the sense that we are in charge, in control, masters of the situation. We get into the habit of taking the responsibility – or rather the credit – for any pleasure, that is allegedly given or sustained, and we hold one another responsible – blame one another – for the pain, that is allegedly caused. In truth nothing is given and nothing is caused because everything still happens but we have managed, by being sociable, to fool ourselves and one another into believing that we are behaving and acting responsibly in a real situation.

From this point of view therefore society is itself a symptom of irresponsibility and a sign of unreality. In reality, while we suppose we "have our reward", we are only prolonging the agony and intensifying the eventual catastrophe.

*

4

This, however, is not the only point of view. What we need to imagine now is a willingness by someone to extract himself from the morbidly pleasurable state of collective irresponsibility. He may be minded to do this because he senses the looming disaster or because he finds the morbidity distasteful, but the more fundamental reason for his desire for detachment is bound to be either reason itself or else desire itself. It will not be a reason or desire for this or that.

I can easily imagine myself, for example, while perplexed and in confusion over these contrary attractions and directions in myself, being on the one hand very capable indeed of fellow feeling and of a supreme loneliness, especially in a crowd and on the other hand very much repelled by that collective spirit, which promises but does not deliver or hold. Indeed this spirit always seems to take away with one hand much more than it offers in the other. The chagrin at being so frequently cheated of my supposed right to companionship and friendship gradually undermines my trust that I will ever be understood, so I surround myself with a shell of independence and self-sufficiency. Betrayal hurts and I cannot help myself but I feel I am being betrayed.

However in my protective shell the longing for true friendship only increases. It can seem unbearable. Can it be true that no one else is like me?

The key to an understanding of my failure to achieve 'satisfactory relationships' does of course lie hidden in my own misunderstanding of what true friendship is all about. I am convinced that I will gain it with someone who is like me – with someone I like and who in turn likes me.

So what am I like? I am like flotsam drifting on a stream. I am like a ravenous beast, injured and sick, unable to obtain nourishment. I am like a clown without an audience, crouching before a cracked mirror and I have run out of face paint. I am like a sophisticated piece of machinery that might be put to good use but no one comes along to use it. I am like someone who wants to live but sees only death all around

6

him. Finally I am like someone who cannot find anyone or anything to compare himself to and the very notion of companionship is being burnt out of me by frustration, disappointment and fear.

The answer to the question: 'What am I like?' finally seems to be: 'Like no one and nothing' and perhaps after a time of artful comparison I will be able to bear it, that within my innermost core I am truly unique. Lucky for me if I live at a time when contemporary art flourishes. However all too often contemporary is a misnomer for the merely temporary. Temporary art caters to the society based on morbid pleasure and the hatred of pain and death. It underwrites the mistaken belief that collectivism is worthwhile and that in ignorance of merciful good spirit we can be real. Such art can only make my uniqueness seem more unbearable.

The critic no doubt will argue that I am wrong to begin with, when I expect any benefit from those I like and from those who like me and of course he is quite right but that's all he is, since he certainly isn't helpful. The 'social critic' has 'seen through' it all, he is no longer fooled and if he advocates anything at all it rarely amounts to more than 'constructive disillusionment'. Compared to him the 'socialist' at least tries to make an honest go of a lost cause. Is that any better?

*

5

The sheer volume of soul-pain I am able to put up with, before I run for cover in some drug-induced state, will determine how likely I am to countenance reason itself or desire itself. Countenancing reason itself implies, in my approach to others and in my reception of them, an awkwardness of such intensity that I may well hesitate before leaving my shell. This is because reason itself, right away, upon my first entertaining it as a possible motivation, inspires in me a seemingly inescapable penchant for dialectical maneuvering. Whatever I experience shows me two faces, not just one and so I feel obliged in conscience either to set one against the other or else to aim at some union of the two.

Why should reason as sole motivation have this effect? As soon as I think, I am beset by contradictory persuasions that would stop me from thinking. In short, I am beset by doubt. Upon close scrutiny it turns out that doubt strikes at me only when I begin to think one thing or another—to think this or that. When I think of leaving my room, it right away occurs to me that the prospect is risky but when I think of staying put I become persuaded, even as I think this, that my health will suffer. When I try to think some problem through, it evaporates and as soon as I let myself think I may be done with it, that perhaps it never really existed in the first place, it looms insurmountable.

The choice presents itself: Give up on reason, on useful thinking, or else just think for the time being, without thinking this or that.

Hopefully it will occur to me that 'just thinking' is an option, that it can be done. With a bit of luck I will be among those who, in spite of my awkward behaviour and attitudes, give me hope. If I become hopeless, I will give up on reason and thought. Doubt at this stage cannot be tackled. I haven't the wherewithal. Every positive suggestion made to me breaks in half and the two halves quarrel.

There are three ways of giving up on reason, so that doubt will no longer plague me. These are force, magic and oblivion. In the absence of hope, when thinking as such or reason itself are bound to seem silly and absurd to me, I begin to toy with magic, to apply force, to seek oblivion. The soci-

ety described earlier, which we can label as Society, makes
all these available in a variety of forms and guises.

*

6

Let's look at the magic first. The word itself is practically meaningless nowadays and not only where English is
spoken. Superficially we associate it with an emotional
pleasure, certainly with a relief of sorts, temporary relief from
worry, also from the horror of the vacuum.

The thing at stake is our sanity, our immediate belief in
the possibility of prolonged existence even though we are cut
off from reality by the very doctrine of hopelessness. I have
no notion at all, not even a hopeful one, of bountiful human
nature, of eternal nourishment, of absolute providence tailored to my unique, individual requirements and needs.
Whence this magic, therefore, that seems to be telling me, to
be urging me: Come back to hope – here is something in the
meanwhile, something to hold on to while you think about it,
even though you will find it, at every step, shrouded in impossibility, at every turn a vexing disappointment ...? Maybe
after all I shall be able to walk through that wall, to make the
pebble in my hand disappear, to float into space with no
strings attached ... The magic is an Ersatz companionship,
after aloneness has turned into isolation. Because I do not
really believe, I am willing to be gulled, as if this were better
than nothing. Scientifically speaking, matter and energy become vaguely interchangeable. Solids dissolve, ghosts
harden, machines become lively, the person next to me ver-
bally grinds on like a rusty thresher.

In one sense the world of magic is ready to welcome me
with open arms. Reinvest your hope, it says, in this endless
cycle of promises of astonishing marvels and wonders that will

raise you in your isolation above all else, so that many will look up to you with admiration, adulation, applause. Think of the fan mail, the prizes, the sheer celebrity of your glamorous status! Think of the gratitude coming your way because you have helped millions to replace their doubtful existence with a dependency on gadgets, with a craving for consumer goods and the possibility of being able to afford them all if only they commit themselves to this straight-line development, this growth principle, in the direction of a final liberty they will gladly mistake for freedom.

So much in one sense.

In another sense, coldly calculating, I tolerate this world of magic, with its immense technological sophistication and its pervasive appeal in every walk of life and I view it as a kind of backdrop against which I will someday be able to imagine a substantial me, a being no longer undermined and degraded but supported and valued, who knows why or how.

This in itself is of course a new hope. Why do I adopt this attitude of detachment towards the magic rather than enlisting my self in its ranks?

I just do. It is given to me to do so, I cannot take credit for it. I can plainly see the risk of stepping across the line and choose not to do so simply because I choose not to do so. Comparing deliberation never enters into it. It's as if I were endowed with an instinct for spiritual survival, whatever that might be.

I don't mind the magic as I opt for meaning.

*

7

In a third sense, magic can become internalized for me as I react to it. I see the flashiness, the charisma, the lack of foundation, of substance, and I hate that, perhaps to the extent that my hatred becomes an obsession. I become a fundamentalist. I make a thing out of my hatred of magic. As a consequence of course I become magical myself. A perception of magic will cling to me even against my will and the very people I despise will seek out my company. This drives me even further into myself and eventually into hatred of myself.

The Draconian measures required for making me 'see sense' are not available in Society, where force, magic and oblivion are after all the rule. I would have to exert myself to overcome the appeal of magic to my vanity. But why would I bother? As a 'member of society' I find that my unreasonable behaviour is amply sanctioned. My absurdities make the front page of the tabloids and my private life no longer yawns back at me. I may be isolated but it doesn't feel like it and that's the main thing.

There is one catch only and that is that I no longer grow and that I cannot fool myself about that. A niggling doubt, an anxious preoccupation with my appearance in public, an increasing fascination by the obscene and the grotesque, a certain political aloofness that collapses at the merest touch of a sentiment, also an impatience with mechanical processes, with machines, that verges at times on madness – all this serves to draw my attention to myself as a sensible being rather than to my self as a magical potency and so I exert myself in the true interest of myself. I do not mean self-exertion but an exertion of myself. The difference between the two, as will become clearer in the following pages, makes for the difference between Society, which is a myth, and society, which is not a myth.

*

11

When I exert myself I want to be and I want to be more. I am fed up with the way my existence seems to be slipping out of my hands. An act of will is what this amounts to. If I am ever to be capable of the society that is not merely a veil drawn over my lack of response to reason but something noble and productive I will have to distance myself from the Society that amounts to magic, force and oblivion.

I do want to distinguish society from Society. I notice this odd complacency in myself and at the same time a sense of outrage. Probably I have it all wrong but often I have the feeling that others have planned my life out for me and in a way that utterly ignores my own tastes and opinions. It's as if it were expected of me to fit into a pattern, to define myself in terms of an abidance with predictable rules and regulations. There are those nearby who seem content with that. How is that possible, I wonder. When I touch on the subject they have no idea what I mean. This scares me. I seem to be the odd one out. I make a point of adapting to what I perceive to be the status quo, I try to 'fit in' but suddenly it's as if something in me snapped and I have to escape.

The solution to my problem evidently does not lie with those around me. It's no good blaming them. It's no good blaming the current government administration either, for this particular problem. The point is, if I amount to nothing, why does it bother me so much? Why am I not peacefully dispersed among the elements? It's perfectly obvious that the world is patterned and arranged and that everybody seems to know what they dislike and they hate it. They are not eaten up inside by self-doubt, their day is not one endless stream of complications. Is it any wonder I bulge with envy? I too want to be careless and free and ready for anything.

The paper moon is not cut out to lead me into romance either. It disgusts me how I get on, silently sighing and lamenting. Sex in society seems so perfectly straightforward. You do as you please, you get on with it. I try it and right away there is trouble. Secret longings obscure the daylight and pursue me into my dreams. Haphazard relationships flare up, then come to nothing. It frightens me, the way I am nearly incapable at times of controlling my urges and I behave absurdly; I frighten others.

As soon as I exert myself, my imagination clears somewhat. However I barely notice myself doing that at first because barely have I started when self-exertion takes over. A reasonable bystander would describe it like this: You say to yourself "I am" and that makes good sense. You say to yourself that irrespective of what you know and experience so far of society, "I am" and that, for the moment, creates a definite order in your immediate vicinity. The inward pressure eases, the outward vexations retreat.

Then something else happens. In my eagerness to perpetuate this ease, this feeling of liberation from the incessant existential harping and drumming, I react forcefully. In retrospect, I wonder why I bother. If the result to my saying 'I am' was ease and clarity, why should it suddenly be useful to insist on a state of such ease and clarity?

That is after all what force in this case amounts to: an insistence by someone on a perpetual state. Surely that cannot always be wrong! When I have found something nice and pleasant, am I not smart to hang on to it, to possess it, to fend off any challenger of my right? In the face of a threat to the flow of essential oil from the Gulf, would it not be stupid of me to sit back and say: Ah well, someone else must need it more than I do? One of the so-called Desert Fathers, was it Macarius in Egypt, on returning to his cell surprised a thief

13

and helped him make off with his belongings, blessing the Lord.

Is it better to punish or to appease the aggressor? Or does humility ever recognize an aggressor? Even more to the point, can I be humble on behalf of those who have elected me to office to represent them in support of their self-interest?

*

9

The magic that makes up a third of society can perhaps be simply described as fidelity to appearances for their own sake, unavoidably at the expense of substance. As I allow myself to be drawn into that magic circle, I notice that whatever integrity I possessed becomes dangerously unreliable and my sense of being human seeps out of me. I grow up as a member of a family in which at best lip-service is paid to the truth. In other words, I am 'raised' on no other basis than in terms of vain regard for the vanity of others. I am educated for many years with due regard to my ability to assert and to aggrandize my self, within a context of half-baked notions of personal charisma and moral platitude. In short, I face the world in ignorance. I am appalled by the prevalence of magic and eventually, in revolt, I exert myself and say that 'I am'. Whatever else may be the case, 'I am'.

What happens?

I enjoy a moment's respite. Any creative act, no matter how anonymous or contrary to convention, is a way of saying: 'I am', 'I count', 'I matter'. Amazing how much assurance this gives me right away! Until now, everyone else seemed to have the advantage. Suddenly I am the only one who is right.

This is marvellous. I do appreciate this sense of myself as of value. I must take steps so that I will never lose track of that. So I exert my *self*. I *insist* on my value. I advertise it and defend it. My first mistake was to be taken in by magic. My second mistake is to use force. I rely on force to make others accept, at least to make them pretend to accept, me as someone to be reckoned with.

Momentarily I became detached from society. Suddenly I am mixed up in it again, in the forceful third of it.

*

10

Self-exertion is the use of force to gain an end. I turn against my own better interest as soon as I use force and yet at such times I feel I do most to advance my cause. While I judged all by appearances, entranced by magic, nothing so much intrigued me as the way those around me were swayed by one word today and the opposite word tomorrow. A friend would please me and I pleased him and nothing came of our friendship because the next day brought mutual displeasure. At that time I could not imagine how force might cure this. Were we not after all at liberty to be swayed as the wind blew?

However now that a genuine bond has sealed our friendship, should I not take steps to guarantee the strength of it? Should I not hedge it round with safeguards to make breakdown less likely?

I exerted myself and love entered my heart. I saw that I am; should I not now insist on it? The love that had entered my heart has made me feel right and powerful but none will admit as much. Even the one I love takes pains to humiliate me, to 'make me wrong'. She employs such subtleties as cause me much grief, hence I set out to invest my affections elsewhere. I know now what it means to feel love and affection, for one and all. It is a vague sense of well-being that surrounds me when I profess my inclination, my good will and charity for one and all. Really I must invent rules and regulations to fasten that sense of well-being down. Never again will I judge by mere appearances but instead by this sense of goodness in me. Whatever would take that from me shall be banned. I will call it bad. If it would remove my sense of goodness it must be bad.

In the meanwhile the love that has entered my heart is like a thing stillborn. I am far too busy at first defining my enemies to notice this. Of course at the same time I define my friends, who make me feel I am better rather than worse. The more I insist on the difference between friend and foe in accordance with this energetic presence in myself of self-esteem, self-confidence and self-assertion, the more does this precious feeling of well-being, this essence of goodness, turn into self-righteousness, so that I tolerate the society only of those who agree with me, who pander to my whims, who swear they depend on me for my good will. Does it not make sense that we should form a party of the like-minded? Is this not how faction is instituted, whereupon conspiracy thrives?

It's a worst-case scenario I describe, I know that, but my intention is to describe the danger and to pinpoint the risk. A detachment from the magic of society is a battle won but the war is not over. Besides, this sense of my goodness which I keep harping on about even while making diverse shows of modesty and self-denial, what is it in the end except another mere appearance, except that now I am inwardly, not outwardly, enthralled? I suppose inasmuch as I have discovered an inward dimension to myself I have made some progress. Love, as it must, has moved me inwardly where before

I could only be moved outside. However now I betray this love as I proceed forcefully, dictating circumstances, insisting on conditions and rights. It's unfortunate, because unwise. I am to be pitied.

*

11

The illusion of being right and the delusion of being good cannot mask for long my predicament. I am being traumatized by a distinct sense of failure. Often it overwhelms me in the midst of some apparent success. Calculation of the odds concentrates the mind for a while before it veers off again to imagine some blessed domain where I no longer have to struggle to prove myself, to keep up standards, to hold together the band of 'the good and the true' who confirm my image of myself as someone who at worst does no harm but at best is a force for change, perhaps even of beneficial change. I subscribe to the 'drop in the bucket' theory to justify my exhausting contributions to what I now see as society, as the company of the like-minded who are not only out for pleasure but for a sense of duty, for the achievement of corporate goals. We stand, we don't loll about. We stand for civilization, for law and order, for the survival of the fittest. Fitness is gained by concerted action in the name of fatherland, 'patrie', patriotism, on the basis of humanitarian principles or a passage from some Holy Book. Society, our Society, has become more of an idol now and my vague longing for togetherness and fellowship becomes perhaps more obsessive, more strained and insistent; enthusiasm may turn into zealotry, I may even try to terrorize those around me into seeing the world as I do, because I know I am right and good and God is on my side. Why should I not force my fellow man to see the light, by crusading against him, by making him adopt my faith on pain of death and destruction, by blowing him up en masse, the cursed infidel and if need be myself along with him? My cause is just. How do I know it's just? It feels like it. How could anything feel so right and yet be wrong!

By fighting for it I make my cause appear even more just, is that not the way it works? If I am willing to fight for it, to die for it, I must be, must be seen to be, on to a good thing.

But force only distorts the mirror. Eventually I become incapable of reflection. I have surrounded myself so diligently with the products of my anxiety, I have defined so closely my idea of good-neighbourliness, my doctrine of social protocol and anathema, of "totem and taboo", that my righteousness is bound to turn sour and the demons begin to tuck at my hem and coat sleeves. My following falls away, I lose faith in 'the faith'; once again I touch the void.

This time, since I imagined I was right and good, it's bound to turn out that I am wrong and bad. It's a terrible thing to have to admit because very likely my 'standing in society' is somehow tied up with this. However I can no longer make ethical ends meet. If I but knew it, I am beginning to rise out of my error. My attitude towards my fellow man is becoming less arrogant. Such weakness overcomes me at times that I feel I must turn to another mortal for help, I, who until recently have been the self-assured dispenser of grace and bounty!

This sense of weakness and helplessness gradually replaces and supplants my sense of being good and right. Forceful self-righteousness, having left behind a trail of destruction of one sort or another, simply peters out.

What I can do now is wallow in self-pity. I can also build up a great stock of resentment. No one appreciates me. No one deserves me.

Or I can again, as before, exert myself. I have learned that self-exertion, being forceful, is not the same as exerting myself, so this time I can exert myself circumspectly. I can say to those around me: You may take me as I am or leave me, I will no longer try to solicit your affection, to earn your regard, to deserve your gratitude. After all it is within me, not within your perception of me, that my value and worth must lie. Never mind how it feels, just so long as it is.

It seems I have learned something important. Something does not have to seem in order to be, to appear in order to exist. I can step up to my fellow man and offer him myself now, because now I know the difference between myself and my self. I no longer insist on who I am and what I amount to but I trust that in good time all will be revealed.

Something has been added to my inward dimension. Call it the principle of growth. I feel all right now about letting relationships begin slowly and develop. It's not up to me to engineer an image of myself. It appears that as soon as I know and acknowledge that I am, I am sufficiently functional, socially, to arouse in those around me a similar showing of who they are and what they amount to. I make some interesting discoveries. Some of those who appeared to be my friends are in truth only sycophants. All that hail-fellow-well-met companionship finally doesn't amount to a hill of beans when compared to the way we can communicate when we let our masks slip a little; when we confess how prone we are to enforcing our will and mistaking this for virtue.

So not only do I say to myself that I am now, but I say it to you too. However in an important sense I leave it at that. I don't try to persuade you against your will that I am. If you don't accept me, I accept there isn't much I can do about that.

If you don't like me, I am not going to change just to please you – which is not the same, is it, as not liking you.

19

I know that I am and I offer you myself and you either accept me or you don't, or perhaps you accept me to an extent. It's what I do in the face of your complete or partial non-acceptance that seems to matter now and I admit it can cause me great difficulty.

*

12

It's eminently worth looking at the love we feel compared to the loving we undertake. When I feel love in your presence I am liable to suppose that I feel it due to you and although I may not right away suppose that you love me, I do feel somehow justified in suggesting to myself that I do love you. All that I have to go on is a feeling. That sounds like a mere thing, when expressed like that. However it can be so intense as to be overpowering.

A feeling is something that happens to us, we don't do it. And yet this is probably the most important thing that *can* happen to us.

Descriptions of this feeling of love abound. Expressions of it are even more numerous. In verse and song we have celebrated this happening throughout the ages. Periodically the interest we take in it seems to eclipse most other cultural concerns. Nevertheless in our private lives we may be troubled by it, in turns fearing it and longing for it.

I know that I myself find the onset of this feeling most unsettling. To the degree that I stand for something or represent it in public, I am shaken. I can find neither rhyme nor reason for this essentially incomparable sensation and for that very reason I find myself trying to deal with it in standard fashion, according to some tried and tested plan – so naturally I fail.

There are two aspects of this I intend to investigate here, rather heartlessly or stupidly you may say, depending on your attitude to 'romance', and they are falling in love and failing in love.

By no means are they both the same, though there is a connection.

Central to my previous success, when I exerted myself knowingly, aware, upon painful experience of failure, of the difference between that and self-exertion, was my ability, learned and practiced, to let it suffice that 'I am', in your presence and in the social vicinity, the society, of others. Force, contract, regulation – proved self-destructive, in the most accurate sense of the word. Consequently I gave up on that and resigned myself – reassigned myself – to the worth-while business of being myself. Companionship, fellowship, was no longer something I was going to 'make happen', by entering into a contract, by joining a club or a society, by in-stituting a foundation or a church.

In a way now both the magical and the forceful aspect of Society lay behind me. Watchfully, wakefully and atten-tively I could make fairly certain of that.

In the midst of success I noticed an unmistakable rest-lessness in myself. I was not getting ahead. Why should I want to get ahead? What was wrong with staying put, with enjoying the fruits of my success? I was no longer being pes-tered by unwanted attentions, no one was making demands on me they had no right to make. I was even blessed with a small circle of acquaintances who seemed to be as prepared to be themselves in my presence as I was prepared to be my-self in theirs. Mostly it was a case of be and let be and be-yond that a watchful eye out for the enemy, the inclination to force and magic and all that that entailed.

It wasn't enough. It hurt me terribly to be rejected when I was being myself. I could cope with having my forceful advances rejected because that was a challenge and it fired my resolve, my ambition for vain investment. My ego and my ambition were not one and the same, so that a setback was peripheral, unimportant, in comparison to my willingness to overcome all odds – while not being myself.

The restlessness returned. Again and again it returned. I must admit that it was frowned upon among my acquaintances, who felt they deserved a quiet life. They were who they were and they were not restless, or so it seemed to me. I needed to get away. I became antisocial. They found me unbearable, insufferable.

I needed to grow. Did they not need to grow? Apparently not. I knew now it would be foolish of me to try to change them. However in their presence I could no longer remain who I was in their eyes: affable, agreeable, tolerant to a fault. It was in their presence, strangely, that the restlessness assailed me most intensely and I behaved in ways that I hated afterwards. Why could I not be like they were, 'perfect in every way'?

Undermined and beset by shame and resentment I avoided their company and went in for the solitary existence. I too wanted the quiet life and it was obvious I could not find it among those who had seemingly achieved it.

The attractions of peace and quiet are strong in direct proportion to the trials, troubles and turmoil we have undergone. Who can say with a certainty that now is not the time to relinquish our hold upon a stressful discipline, for the enjoyment of well deserved rest? How can we call ourselves human and creative if unwilling to search and discover afresh the personal and universal truth relevant to our individuality and our time?

So I remained indecisively and agonizingly suspended for a time, as it were between mutually exclusive powers. On one side the solitary existence beckoned, with all those vividly imagined opportunities for uninterrupted study, for languid meditation and contemplation, for the continued enjoyment of my victory over the magic and force of society, the prejudice in the face of mere appearances and the insistence on making my presence felt, on impressing my self upon an often all too willing or unwilling world. This solitary existence would be my final victory, in terms of something I pictured as a kind of self-development, and it would be the defeat of this restlessness, of this very threat to my newly discovered inner being of myself, which I knew now could not be sustained through self-exertion.

On the other side I was willing to entertain the possibility of immersing myself in a welter of abstract business: abstract because the connection with any particular practical reality seemed almost beside the point, since distraction was what would make the difference between being hounded and ... not being hounded.

My reaction to this persisting agony of restlessness could therefore be summed up as an uneasy combination of – an apprehensive vacillation between – self-development and self-immersion.

*

13

However it seems that love is not calculable. I continue to speak in the first person singular here because it allows me to draw on personal experience in a more exemplary fashion but the indefinite pronoun, one, would serve even better. So for example: One is lucky to get away from the terrors of exposure to society with his hide in tact. Or: One prospers in

23

society to the detriment of his soul. One has vanquished the instinct for popularity and is left with nothing to do.

*

14

The self-development and the self-immersion is what I mean by <u>oblivion</u>, by the third aspect of society. I am wondering now, since I am already distinguishing Society from society, would it not be smarter to speak of three disguises or masks rather than aspects, keeping in mind however that when you take the masks away there is nothing left? Or perhaps we should say that there are three ways of hiding from reason (and desire) and mistaking them for society: magic, force and oblivion.

It is the unidentifiable restlessness that keeps surfacing when I slow down in my mechanical pursuit of some endless achievement in which I am involved with many others and we all agree that it won't do to cease in our effort, whatever the outcome. We all immerse ourselves in the collective effort. If someone lets the side down he is somehow made to feel it. The threat of the transcendental restlessness is not a joking matter. While it is feared it gives rise to antisocial behaviour, or more correctly anti-Social behaviour. There is no need to fear it but we fear it all the same, mostly because we don't know any better. On that side of the equation, the self-immersion side, I would have to learn how to be quiet and sit still until I realized that there was nothing to fear.

But of course it's usually not as easy as that. I am all the more committed to my evasive tactics because I am convinced I am fleeing from an enemy. The idea is to blot out any suspicion of being wrong about this. Hence the utopia of the popular society, the Society, where everything ticks over with perpetual mobility, the effect of magic, force and oblivion.

24

So I try to live, in fear of reason, restless from raw, uninvested desire, committed to a social contract that supposedly guarantees eventual success. In many ways oblivion is usually the last stage before a Society breaks down, before it disintegrates, before it is amalgamated in, or absorbed by, another Society. This other Society is then, often in retrospect, judged to have been stronger, more able, which means that more of its members, or elements, are more magically and forcefully committed. It's a peculiar shift of emphasis when we speak of Societies rather than of Society, because Society is ideal, pertaining to the realm of ideas, while Societies presumably exist or else existed, or are brought into existence.

None of this makes much sense of course unless we compare it to what I intend to discuss and describe eventually as society, with a small s, within the context of 'association' of both those who do not rely on magic, force and oblivion and those who do.

*

15

But how can self-development be seen as an attempt to become oblivious to reason and desire?

It seems understandable enough, especially from an essentially sympathetic point of view, that self-immersion, my immersion of my self in both things and the pursuit of things, as part of the hectic or dogged ambition to rise above the fear of death, might be a mistaken way of escape from the strangeness, the utter otherness, of reason. Surely self-development, by comparison, is positive, is creative, is reasonable and desirable!

Outside of me, I fear, are all these 'things'. They confuse me; they make unreasonable, unseasonable demands on me; they make me feel insecure, impotent, small. I rise to the occasion. I categorize and control them, I coerce them into subjection, I enslave them. I legislate, I rule and regulate, not changing a thing in truth but bringing the lot of them under my supremacy, my state sovereignty. In this way I manage to some extent, for periods of time completely, to ignore my own developing ego, to ignore, that instead of a soul I have a self now, which is to all intents and purposes yet another 'thing'. I cannot conquer the world and preserve my soul, someone should have told me that.

What does it really amount to now, if I turn away from the welter of things outside, all of which only exist for me because I have not begun to perceive beings but mistake them for what they are not, namely labeled things – if I turn away from that, from this and that, from "the thousand things", and towards the thing that is my self, and develop that? If I become fanatical about goodness, say, how am I different from the one who amasses a thousand things?

*

16

My self-development would begin with my desire to conquer restlessness. But what is this restlessness other than pure, clear desire announcing itself? Reason is among us and so is desire. My eyes remain closed to both. The master, who has until now taught me as it were in absentia, would like me to rise to his level. We should see eye to eye. This implies a change for me, I needn't kid myself. Secretly I wish to remain under tutelage. Let others make my decisions for me, then I can blame them for my mistakes.

So that is the meaning, the purport, of this essential, 'endless' restlessness. So I desire to replace it, to move something into its stead – my self. This self is the idea I have of myself, or the image. Now is the time for positioning it fairly

26

and squarely within a gilt frame. (In a dream it is revealed to me as a *guilt* frame, what they call a frame-up on the street.)

The question, the sober and conscientious question, is: Whence do I take the desire to cheat desire? I have no doubt that I do desire to be rid of this endless, meaningless restlessness. How mistaken I am and how much in error!

I wish not to be reminded of my dire proximity to the truth about myself. The truth about myself is that I am so close to freedom that I can smell it and so nearly out of the clutches of Society that an absent-minded wriggle would finish the job and yet that is what frightens me – but forgive me, for I cannot picture the terrain on the other side of the wall.

I am nearly there. What remains is the remainder, the rest. Who can imagine the terrain on the other side of Society? Let us instead once again agree, in this way we have of agreeing as Social beings, to yet another cover-up. Let us agree to manufacture the rest on this side, on the inside. Let there be a consensus in regard to the truth of the matter, that we play cowardly games in dark corners with our backs to the light.

The desire for self-development is therefore a sham. Self-development is a cowardly act but the desire for it is a sham because it is really a wish to be no longer reminded of our dangerous proximity to freedom from Society.

*

17

Shall we take a peak through a chink in the wall? Look, this invisible rough surface is the wall and where I hold my fingers thus, here you may peek. Can you for a moment forget about your oh so developed self and risk even a sidelong glance at what I propose to show you?

Here is the rest, among some of those who have taken the pains to make it out. Their desire was blessed so that yours might benefit from benediction. No, you have nothing to fear from exposing your ignorance to theirs, your wisdom to theirs.

Know they exist. This is worth knowing. Expect no advertisement, no promotion or presentation in the political sense. How would you like to imagine them? As the community of the faithful? Careful now, guard against ingrained prejudice. We must use words you have heard before. Sometimes entire phrases glitter in a new light. You too have collaborated, as we all have, in the self-justifications of society. We have allowed this mass idol to come into being. Instead let <u>us</u> be. Let <u>us</u> exert ourselves and forget about the idol. I cannot make it any plainer at the moment.

*

18

The hole in the wall trick is to let you know what you have to crawl through if this last vestige of Society is to fall away from you. You will know nothing of society until you have rid yourself lock, stock and barrel of your commitment to force; until the magic of the 'divine surface' has been peeled away for you like the skin of a snake; until the oblivion of self-immersion and self-development have become for you a raging storm in which you will not entrust your barque to the sea. Actually I don't think you have much of a chance. You are so attached to your mistakes, you have made such a life-task out of justifying them, that a major obstacle such as your sense of self, arrogant or pathetic, is really what you pray to, to improve yourself, so that what you seek is self-improvement. I hope this is making you angry. Would you like to prove me wrong?

So who is this 'community of the faithful'?

28

What sort of a question is that? What do you mean: Who is it? It's all those who are, have been and will be faithful. They are in community. They are also in communication, it cannot be otherwise. Be faithful and right away be in communication with them.

How many are there? I haven't a clue. It's not at all important. Everything to do with number has to be thought away from them. Everything to do with name has to be thought away from them. The community of the faithful is a concept and an image. You are not going to get anywhere trying to pin either one down. You are not going to get anywhere unless you stop trying to get behind my strategy here. I simply speak from experience. I tell you nothing I have not tasted and seen.

It stands to reason that when we move through a fog we have to fix our mind on something.

*

19

I have recalled, for the purpose of edification, that aspect of the concourse of women and men that does us no credit but entraps and enslaves us, so that we no longer know either ourselves or one another and are fastened down, out of reach of our human destiny, by desires that betray desire and by reasons that mock reason. Surely no vast commentary on the affairs of mankind is required to illustrate, to a satisfactory degree of clarity, how we may be duped, in our association, by our own laxity or enthusiasm and how a little wisdom at the right moment can restore us to a regard for one another that leaves judgement and condemnation to a higher power as we concentrate on our natural love of what is good and true. We are born with that love as a capacity and as an ability that needs only to be recognized and acknowledged and then invested in deed.

Once we begin to seek within ourselves, we have found. It creates a difficulty, that we hope to recognize within ourselves what we have constructed outside on no sound basis. The purpose of the search is not to find what we know but to know what we have.

One thing we have is affinity for one another. This affinity is a strong link once we confess it but it vanishes immediately upon insistence. During the course of the most rudimentary conversation we may confess this affinity or we may insist on it, the choice is always and every time my own and yours.

The confession of this natural human – or human natural – affinity does not always come easy but it is never more effective than in despite of an antipathy or dislike. Its effectiveness at any time is measurable in terms of antipathy and dislike overcome. In their absence we can see clearly where we stand in relation to someone. It is this relation which is of the essence. It is essential that we see clearly and know certainly how at a given time we stand in relation to someone. My own business of course is to know how I stand in relation to you. It is not my business to know how you stand in relation to me, if at all. That is for you to decide.

One can hardly overstate the importance of minding one's own business in this case of achieved clarity and certainty over present relationship by way of a confession of human natural affinity. To the extent that we mind one another's business we trespass. If we neglect to appreciate the seriousness of such trespasses, such as the crippling effect they have on our natural affinity, we will not be capable of society in the end.

20

What does it mean, to confess one's human natural affinity? How can I do that? I have nowhere to lay blame except myself. I curb my enthusiasm and control my high spirits. Whether I am glad or not glad to see you, to talk to you, to do business with you, this does not touch on the affinity I mean. It has no bearing on what I am to confess. Whatever I sense, without or within myself, has nothing to do with it. This is important for me to know so that I am not sidetracked. Neither is there any need to deny what I sense or feel. What matters is simply that I look elsewhere, that I turn aside from sensations and feelings and keep searching. The determined, patient search will eventually bring me to my goal.

How will I know that I have arrived and that the search has turned up what I set out to find?

That is not a relevant question in this context. I am not looking for a thing, or for a particular sensation or feeling, or for an answer to a question, a solution to a problem. Or rather, I may be doing something like that too but then at the same time I confess my human natural affinity, for which I search, for your sake and my sake, both.

In a way, therefore, it's the search that counts. It is something I am definitely doing while I am in some relation or communication with you. I am letting you know thereby that I myself know of my human natural affinity, that I know that it is and that it can come into existence and also that I am at the present time willing to enter into a human natural relationship with you, whatever else I am hoping to gain from our time together. In fact whatever else I hope to gain, I will, in the final analysis, be wasting my time unless it is human naturally based.

My 'confession', to you, could therefore be described as my willingness to let you know that I am aware of my human natural affinity, as a capacity, and that I am desirous of bringing it into existence, for our benefit. It cannot fail to be for my own benefit, this confession and unless you actively throw it back in my face somehow or else have sunk into a matchless state of callousness, it is bound to work also to your advantage, perhaps not now and here but then later.

I don't think it's unhelpful to speak of it as a confession. What we are wise to recall again here is that what happens, automatically, when two or three of us get together, is selfishness. That is the normal and predictable reaction, when we meet, merely on account of our being individually unique. When water droplets meet there is at first an increase of surface tension in each, before they merge. Distrust happens, and so does enchantment, fascination. It amounts to the same, in that we have not initiated it and therefore it is not human naturally based. I dealt with this more elaborately in a previous book where I equated misery and happiness in comparison to blessedness or bliss. The former come about automatically, the latter is a response to something done. In this present study, where the emphasis is not on religion but on society, what is intentionally done, in particular, is this confession. And it is done – it has to be done – in spite of what happens and quite irrespective of all happy or unhappy commotion under which we may be labouring at that moment.

So I take it for granted that selfishness of one sort or another is automatically set off in me as soon as we encounter one another, be it pleasant or unpleasant selfishness, and my confession will therefore be after the manner of a search. While I can take my wickedness for granted, my proneness to

32

evil, far be it from me to take my human nature for granted, since it does not happen but it depends for its existence on my knowledge and acknowledgement of it and on my subsequent investment of particular aspects of it.

Therefore I confess my human natural affinity by searching for it, by keeping in mind that it is readily eclipsed, masked – or even replaced, such as if I were to insist that whatever else happens I am after all a human natural being, with my pride and my rights – in other words if I were to insist that, for example, I am worth knowing and meeting. As soon as I insist, my case collapses. I am only worth knowing and meeting if and while I confess my human natural affinity. Otherwise I am a stumbling block and perhaps one among thousands, as a member of Society.

*

21

It would be wrong now to suggest that human natural affinity makes for the social connection or that it guarantees society. All we can say at this point is that in the absence of such affinity only Society can occur, while society, which does not occur but must be brought about, depends on that affinity.

What we need to do now is differentiate between society and community. It's in our own interest not to confuse the two. When we do, this is no great misfortune but it unduly limits our capacity for life.

The narrow view reveals community as a natural outcome or extension of the search for human natural affinity, which is our confession of faith, so to speak. What we can imagine here is something like a spark that leaps between or among us in its own good time, whereupon we exist on a higher and better level.

This in itself is well worth our attention. Something is going on that is of a new order. If this is not recognized we may end by behaving wastefully. However, as usual, since I cannot dictate what you will do and you cannot decide what I will do, it is up to each one of us to appreciate this new order from his or her own personal point of view.

And the first 'order of the day' of course is to admit that this new order exists. This admission can be readily classified as obedience. It would be on some consciousness of my own obedience to whatever seems appropriate to this order at the time that the next stage of my success depends. In the absence of such obedience it makes no sense for me to suppose that the new or communal order exists for me; in fact I will probably 'kick against the pricks' as it were and try, by hook or by crook, to set up my own, self-conceived order in contradistinction to it. In other words, I will miss the boat.

This reveals community to the wider view, as a new and better order of being, with which we may align ourselves, observantly and obediently.

Perhaps we should not expect it of ourselves that a higher and better order of being should go initially unchallenged by our ego. If anything seems calculated to arouse such egocentricity in us it is such a communal order of being. This can be explained somewhat in terms of the ethical content of this order. Our own lack, or shortfall, of ethical content is highlighted for us. By ethical content I mean the capacity for doing good.

Whenever my own comparative insufficiency is pointed out to me I experience this – perhaps I am bound to experience it – as an infringement of my rights and as an enforcement, by someone else or even by mere circumstances, upon me, of alien rights.

34

This is not to say that no one will ever try to enforce alien rights. We do that all too often ourselves, when we bully one another, either emotionally or by being opinionated. In such a case we are bullied, and feel bullied, by someone who insists on our obedience to his being merely 'other'. This can arouse justifiable anger in us.

So discernment is required, because ego leaps to the fore, unjustifiably, not in response to the 'other' but in automatic reaction to the new, specifically in our present case to a new order of being. What is being held out to us is an ethical improvement or enlargement and in order to be able to take advantage of it we first of all have to conquer that all too familiar surface tension, the mere selfishness.

*

22

We should never tire of reminding ourselves and one another of the impossibility of making someone other than ourselves appreciate and obey that new order. Any attempt to set up an order in which to constrain others to obedience is bound to be self-conceived and in egotistic reaction to the truly new order and its ethic challenge. It is up to the contemporary philosopher to help us discern between the parable and the truth. If I see a lot of well-meaning people wander in the countryside, devoid of food, shelter and hygiene, I may well decide, in a similarly well-meaning fashion, to gather them under a roof, to teach them vegetable gardening and cleanliness. I may call this a community. I can call it anything I like. I may insist that for the sake of orderliness a few rules have to be obeyed and regulations observed. Even such a philanthropic effort, at best, should not, however, be confused with the new order that comes into being as an extension of my confessional search for human natural affinity and which has to be acknowledged obediently by me upon my personal

35

overcoming of my selfish rejection of it. The truly new order has ethical content and it always has more than the one to whom it occurs. A self-conceived 'order', by comparison, may function in terms of a variety of moral constraints but it cannot be said to have ethic content, such as a human person, or of course the new order, always has.

*

23

Several thoughts come to mind here.

We are understandably reluctant to leave Society behind or to one side because after all we do have that, even though it amounts to no more than a series of chance occurrences. In it we have a semblance of community, which can be pleasant at times, so why should we look for more until we actually see better? When the lack of foundation becomes apparent, upon affliction, we blame ourselves, one another, circumstances but not necessarily this ephemeral construct of prejudice and vain hope. Perhaps we retreat from it for a while, into despair of mankind and the world but as soon as someone likes us or we suspect a promise of general popularity we are liable to perk up again, to return to our canine instincts.

For this reason, on account of this understandable reluctance, the rarest occurrence of all is a wholehearted embrace of what I have called the new order. Neither is it a simple matter to describe what such a wholehearted embrace would look like. As a matter of fact whatever aspect of it we suppose we *can* describe must after all be something else. This we can put down to the newness of it. Newness defies description. The more we think about it, the more obvious such a statement becomes. In a thousand and one more or less effective ways we can say what it is like, such as when we write a novel, but we cannot place our finger directly on it.

36

It will be observed and obeyed but not described or explained. However, from within our Social persuasion, observation and obedience have their own peculiar meaning, don't they. A liberated Social individual is apt to look askance at any proposal to obey because he has set himself up as the final arbiter. On close inspection however he can be seen to be a very slave in terms of blind obedience, such as to all his arbitrary stirrings and agitations, his tempers and moods which define his reasons and sanction his chaotic desires. Similarly his observation may go to great lengths for the minutest detail with the aid of the most sophisticated instruments but of service, of the will to serve, one detects precious little. In his curiosity he is perhaps not so much attentive as greedy for the as yet unnoticed. In my hope of enlivening the public domain in the interest of my celebrated self, the raw desire expresses itself to bind me once again and more securely into the Social system.

Little wonder, therefore, that I am so slow to come round to the new order, to that spirit of a new order, that presents itself to me, in timely response to my search for human natural affinity. I have not been able to picture it, so how can I recognize it? Every fibre of me may be alienated, so of course I alienate that spirit and call it strange, unorthodox, heretical.

One historic phenomenon therefore is the wholehearted rejection of communal reality. The meaning of the new order is communal reality. On occasion those who have searched most desperately for the human connection have also become most perfervidly reactionary in their resistance of it when eventually faced by it. Mighty Societies and Social institutions have been based on such perverse motivation. We do well to be on the watch for that. Those who advertise themselves as great benefactors of personal relationship, bolstering their message with diverse mysteries and occult practices,

37

may in truth be the most successful enemies of man's human-natural affinity to man.

When it comes to acceptance rather than outright rejection of this affinity and eventual communal reality, it may be useful to speak of two or three stages or dimensions of it.

*

24

I may not be able to make an outright commitment to communal reality simply because of my make-up, of the way I am created. There are differences of character, of constitution, of temperament which have to be taken into account when we estimate the volitional capacity of a person. It is not a case of: What does this person understand, but of: What does he want.

The realization is the same in all cases. Once we have a genuine insight into, or a taste for, communal reality we exist as it were on a new basis and we share that basis with all others who have gained that knowledge. This makes out what we might call our common heritage. We might describe this by saying that we are once again as we were meant to be at the beginning.

What makes for the above mentioned difference between us is how, and to what extent, we experience the difference between ourselves, that is to say between those who know, and those who do not know. It may make me supremely angry that there are so many who take no interest whatsoever in their own regeneration and they leave themselves open to one destructive influence after the other, for all the world as if human beings were at the mercy of the animal and the machine. They have no sense of honour, they respect nothing, they strive for nothing that is good. It would be a deep-seated anger in me, which would motivate me in my work so that I would confront, provoke and agitate among the children of the darkness who say there is no light and that no one has the right to see it. This anger would be tempered by the sadness I would experience in the face of my impotence as I now and again try to force enlightenment, which is of course out of the question.

Then again I might be such a one who knows this anger well enough but is consumed by the desire to give ample proof, for all the world to see, of the communal experience in all its variety and degrees of intensity, so that those without knowledge of the communal order should as soon as possible take pains and the trouble to know. My motivation, in this case, would not so much be righteous anger but caring love and affection, although the anger would play a role. It would counteract the periodic cooling of affection by revitalizing my body of care.

Thirdly I might find myself urged beyond this to the point where my own personality becomes an aspect of my work, where, so to speak, I want to be what I say and say what and who I am, in the light and context of this new and final communality. I would become increasingly aware of a multi-faceted spiritual commonwealth in which no thing remains untouched by humanity and to which all beings belong by right of their birth. Impressed by this spiritual birthright of all beings and creatures, I would wish above all else, and in addition to my other works, to set a personal example, simply by living to the full what I believe, know and understand. Needless to say the other two dimensions, the anger and the careful love and affection, would play into this. (Each one may be a stage if another follows, or a dimension if we stop there. So the righteous or creative anger and the careful love and affection may be dimensions or stages but the personal example can only be a dimension because one cannot go beyond it.)

*

Communal reality replaces Society. The two cannot co-exist. As soon as we actually experience a genuine affinity, not to our fellow man, who is an abstraction, but to another man, woman or child, we are bound to find Society (not society!) repugnant. What does all this to-do about what is done and what is not done really amount to? What is the origin of all these so-called principles, the basis for all these standards? Superstition and hypocrisy shimmer through everywhere and an intense hatred of the truth!

Knowing that an adherent to the Social order or pattern calls the truth falsehood and falsehood truth is of no help to anyone. However imagine now a young person who grew up in Society and then discovers he is blessed or gifted with a genuine communal experience of affinity and who tries for the first time to communicate that experience. Look what a marvellous thing I have discovered, he will say, his eyes shining! What he anticipates is congratulation and celebration. What he gets, to his consternation, is stony looks, cynical grins, sarcastic comments.

We have to take sides here. Are we on the side of Society, which rightly fears that its arrangements, its framework, its painstaking codification of what is done and what is not done, will become anarchy if these, to its eyes, half-baked notions of brotherly love, of indiscriminate affection for all – if this romance of juvenile enthusiasm takes over? Or are we on the side of the young person who has woken up to the centre of his human being and is bubbling over with naive delight? Obviously something has to give way. The communal reality and Society cannot coexist.

*

Let's have a look at what the young person has discovered. He feels drawn towards those who smile upon him and he is, let's face it, willing to do anything for them. He understands for the first time in his life that the true reality which implies, and corresponds to himself as, a fully alive and whole person is somehow connected to relationship between individual human beings and to co-operation among persons. Not surprising at his age, especially after a period of adolescent aloneness, that he supposes he has woken up to something that everyone around him has always known. A welcome, a celebration by his elders, would not overly astonish him. What he comes up against is in many ways the exact opposite. This can go on over a lengthy period in terms of a great number of trivial incidents which all seem to mount up to bring something home to him or, depending as always on constitution and make-up, the pressure can build in a short time as if to force a showdown of some sort.

What this novice in life does not understand yet is that although the essence of communal reality has been revealed to him, he is not to stop there, with this wonderful feeling- or thought-experience in all its superficiality but to go on to discover in himself the original, live and essentially personal response.

Of course he cannot be expected to feel like doing that. Neither can he be expected to come up with a more realistic appreciation of what has happened to him by thinking about it. Technically, at his present stage of growth, he can either think *or* feel but not both. He can either feel or think very intensely and he may be tempted to do one of these to the detriment or at the expense of the other but he cannot combine them yet. He cannot yet, as it were, play the piano with both hands at the same time.

This is the most crucial moment of a person's life. Since he cannot come upon the ultimate truth of this matter within his feeling or thinking self, it must be taught to him. The essential definition of the teaching process applies here. Someone who knows must tell the one who does not know or the ignorant individual gets stuck. In the absence of this fundamental teaching, the young person is bound to go astray. If no one is around to teach him he will go astray. Although he has been touched by the communal life experience he will not be able to make the appropriate and just sense of it but he will sheer off into a behaviour that is wasteful.

What is it he needs to be taught?

On one hand it must be brought home to him that what he feels or thinks under the influence of this novel experience is not for public consumption or for private indulgence. On the other hand let him take on board that Society's unwelcoming reaction to his novelties of thought and effusions of feeling is, in that case, no more than you would expect and that the pain inflicted upon him compares somewhat to what happens when we put our hand into the fire or our face in the water. It's what you would expect. We might not be willing to thank the flame and the wave, or Society, for instructing us but at least we might learn not to strike back.

So it's important for this young person blessed with communal experience not to try to get back at the various Social forces and their agents for not being good and just. They will be kind enough if he minds his own business, whatever that is, but he mustn't try to interfere with Society's painstaking investment in the conviction that the truth is false and that falsehood is true, that goodness is shallow, that the good as such does not exist, that justice is arbitrary and that the ultimate arbitrator is the largest bank account and the biggest cannon.

*

42

I suppose the burning question for the young person is the following:

What am I to do with this new joy and enthusiasm which no one wants to know about and they either remain sternly indifferent or they behave as if they were afraid I would betray their darkest secret? When I don't express this emotion, this feeling, these opinions and thoughts, I am pressed by a great weight. This depression is terrible. I cannot bear it. I refuse to bear it. Why should I? I know with the certainty of my heart that what bubbles up in me is right and good and it obviously wants to be shared. When no one wants anything to do with it, the pain is awful. The joy turns to resentment. A whole new logic of love and affection, of intimacy and charity presents itself to me, however unrequited it turns into hatred, loneliness and despair. Do I have a choice here? Can anyone suggest an alternative to this urge I have to identify an enemy and to devote my time to combat?

If Society were identified as the enemy, this would be quite correct in a sense. Once I have tasted the truth, he who says there is no truth or who hates the truth is my enemy. However it is how I behave towards this enemy that will make the difference for me. Pain due to unrequited love can seem unbearable. When soul-pain becomes unbearable, how long before a murder is committed? How long before the mind goes into overdrive or the flesh becomes rebellious and illness or sickness sets in?

It would seem obvious that my chief concern should be how I am and not how Society is. If I knew of a way of dealing with this problem of abortive communality, of unrequited love, of endless joy turned into overflowing wretchedness, I would forget all about the enemy for the time being and concentrate on how I am and on what I do. I would smile on Society and pity its card carriers for not knowing what they do, for hating the truth when they really have no notion of it and let's face it, the notion I myself now have of it has not been earned or deserved by me, so would it make sense for me to criticize, judge and condemn those who are ignorant of it?

So it's a gift the young man has. He has to figure out what to do with it. His first attempt to make a go of it didn't turn out too well. Now he has thought things over. He may be disappointed, frustrated, bruised but he is willing to set his ill will aside for the time being in order to review the situation.

Let us take this opportunity to teach him something. Let us teach him that this gift of communal reality is not to be flaunted or squandered. Let us also teach him that the cause of his wretchedness is his animosity towards those who reject him and that it rests entirely with him to rid himself of the wretchedness by substituting general good will for the animosity. This would be a truly creative act. As such it even amounts to a practical investment of his gift. He can direct benevolence whenever he wishes and wherever he wishes and he can do that even while he is most wretched. That's very important. It takes a wise man to understand that we do not have to be rid of the fruits of our wickedness before we can begin to do good but a young man can learn it. He will learn it most readily if he is taught by example.

*

28

The illusion we labour under when we suppose our social function begins and ends with the use we are to others is after all not a bad one, except that it does not make for an investment of our communal gift. We can be brought up in a morality of duty and sacrifice and yet feel totally unfulfilled. When we look at what it means to be young but no longer a child, so that our human nature is no longer in its infancy but not yet the mainstay of our commitment to the well-being and welfare of men, women and children, we come across a certain mysterious quantity, which seems to defy definition while at the same time demanding attention, but a very peculiar type of attention. When we refer to it as youth we usually mean a kind of second nature which reveals itself to us and to those around us as a need, a new need, a need for something different. Describing someone as a young person does not conventionally call to mind this reality of a young nature, which is something quite specific and not to be categorized or classed with human nature or immature nature, or corrupt nature. When human nature is branded as corrupt we have a real problem on our hands. Immaturity does not mean young but refers to spoiled or neglected maturity but there too we have to ask: Is it our nature or is it we ourselves who are corrupt, or immature?

And yet when someone is young we are justified in saying that their nature too is young. This gets us a small step closer to the peculiarity of youth.

Understanding the difference between oneself and one's nature is of course essential. While a confusion exists for us here or while we perhaps even equate the two – if they mean the same thing to us – we are not on the right track at all.

A sizeable amount of preparation is required here before we can track, so to speak, the first social impulse and act, in the case of someone who has come up against the animosity or falsehood of Society and has been thrown back on the gift, as I have advisedly called it, of his communal reality, of his potential and eventual existence on the higher plane and in the new dimension of community. It may prove helpful if after a while we introduce the term 'social community' but at present this would not have much meaning.

*

29

It helps if we have a fair grasp of the so-called 'origin' and 'function' of Society, though that is a loose application indeed of those concepts. Are we to assume that the young person in the making, whose good nature is brimming, has no option but to steer straight into falsehood before he can learn about the truth of himself? Is the alternative a run-in with Society – indeed what is the alternative? Several options, which on closer inspection look more like miscarriages, present themselves, even to the naked eye, if history as she tries to live and breathe is consulted. The romantic interlude is one, a dream-infested parlance among knotted vines and grave-stones, a getting trussed up in morbid introspection, there's at least as much pleasure in that as in wrong-footing Society. The setting-up of an alternative Society is another, with plenty of ideological content to make the world appear conquerable and the earth look small. Thirdly, consider, if you would, the pitting of self against self, splitting the self itself, if you please and stoking the antagonistic hatred resulting, both inside your individual as he bravely tries to exist and among individuals, competing to get to the top of the heap for that first and final crow, underpinned if possible by a plethora of pseudo-Luciferian rubbish. You might say that all the other alternatives partake of the worm-eaten essence of these three and then again you might think better of it by ignoring the lot.

But can the lot in fact be ignored? This too seems legitimate as a question. Is it not rather the painful and therefore not readily acknowledged case that any avoidance of falsehood merely plays into its hands? Whether you fight it or run away from it, you are playing by its rules. In the face of

46

Society (not while part of Society, mind) the morality of fight or flight itself comes a cropper.

So I dare say, that thicket of *Angst* and agony has gradually and laboriously to be worked through. Your ancient Greek hero and your medieval Christian knight share in a common pursuit. Renown is earned and virtue appropriated. In legend and saga it looks well and under conditions at least semi-fictional it works out best. In actual down-to-earth practice things can get a bit messy. Millions starve, are poisoned, the territory is genocidally cleansed of them but that is by the by as long as the rooster gets in that crow and internationalism can be seen to make some headway and the morbid craving finds expression and outlet.

Come to think of it, there may be a genuine alternative. Imagine yourself as a young person growing up in the companionship of those who can see through the Societal falsehood, who see and identify clearly the falseness of Society and instruct you in the investment of your sound human nature, which implies the timely immolation of your self, not through self-sacrifice, public or private, or by way of the morality of fight or flight, but on the basis of faithful knowledge and understanding.

When I say 'faithful knowledge and understanding' I do not ignore the difficulty of differentiating between self-sacrifice and immolation of one's ego or self. Self-sacrifice, if you can take that on board, is itself an exercise of the self while any immolation of our self presupposes our awareness of merciful good spirit as ever-influential reality.

*

30

It's impossible to think of faithful knowledge and understanding, to take it seriously, if this does not include the immolation of one's self, the hatred of it by oneself and if it does not <u>ex</u>clude self-sacrifice. The mix-up between self-sacrifice and immolation of self is endemic to the modern mind-set.

So is the mix-up between the person's human being and his or her nature. Not surprisingly, the two mix-ups testify to the same lack of knowledge and understanding, with the emphasis on faithful in the latter case and on merciful in the former.

It matters a great deal to me, to my wellbeing and welfare, how I think about myself, how I imagine myself and this in turn is very much influenced by my knowledge and understanding of what is a human being. We speak of someone being true to his nature, we praise someone else for being so natural and down to earth. Then we excuse peccadilloes for being, after all, <u>only</u> human nature. Or we say: Human nature being what it is, a given kind of dastardly behaviour is hardly surprising. Then, in some quarters, human nature is considered utterly corrupt. Or alongside the doctrine of the 'noble savage' as an innocent child of nature we have that quite opposite one of natural man as lost, evil and unaware of it.

Merciful knowledge and understanding however reveals human nature as in itself safe and sound but not necessarily known and understood by us as individual human beings. An immature human being, for example, being one who has neglected or abused his maturity, ignores his human nature to some degree, while an immoral human being, for another example, being one who flouts goodness and flaunts wickedness, misunderstands his human nature. Both can be helped by being brought back to their nature, by having their nature, their safe and sound human nature, revealed to them; by having their knowledge of their true nature clarified and ascertained and by having their understanding of it perfected and rendered reasonable. It makes a lot of difference whether those who preach the need to be reborn imply the acquisition or whatever of a different nature or the return to the original one which has been abused, forfeited, betrayed, falsified, ignored, etc. The invention of a supernatural realm is not the same as a reinstatement of human nature, and therefore of all of nature in general, in its true and original right.

This is not to say that nature or human nature is good, which it is not. But neither is it bad. There is, however, a close and strong connection between our safe and sound human nature and our perception of the truth. The worthwhile search for the truth goes hand in hand with the knowledge and understanding of our nature and we need not apologize for that.

So the answer to the question: Who are you and what do you amount to? Tells us nothing about your nature or about human nature in general, though it should indicate how you stand in relation to it. If you are talented, it still makes all the difference what use you make of that talent. If your nature is a burden to you, then quite aside from all clever speculation why this should be so, what it comes down to in the end is whether and how you carry that burden. Your greatest asset meanwhile will be your knowledge of human nature in general as dynamic and live and your understanding of it as something than which you can never be greater, though you may come right up to its greatness. In the particular, when you speak of your nature, and assuming you have the right to do so, you might point to your acquired good habits, to your powers of persuasion in the right quarters, to your ability to deal with failure and success, and such like, always keeping in mind that you yourself, along with your ability to good and your immortality, are wicked and mortal, which is to say prone to evil and liable to die, and that it is your solidarity with human nature, if you diligently maintain and thoroughly sustain it, that assures you quality of character and integrity of person. Therefore keep in mind the good news, that if you have once again committed some idiocy, you have only yourself to blame, which greatly simplifies the required remedial action.

At one time, of course, human nature was – not corrupt but incomplete, waiting, so to speak, for completion. Then it was completed. Since then human nature is whole and all of us who know and understand this, faithfully and mercifully, are whole. The emphasis is therefore on us and on what and how we know and understand.

It is the modern fallacy to search forever in 'nature', human or otherwise, and among natural phenomena, for the hidden or missing link that will explain our culpable actions and our erratic behaviour, as if such explanations could make any odds. We cannot correct or improve nature, not because we aren't up to it but because it needs no correcting or improving, since it is whole. And prior to its wholeness it needed no correcting or improving either, but completion and happily this has been accomplished. Of course we may wish to express our gratitude for this act of completion but does it not perhaps speak most highly for the sincerity of our gratitude if we actually take into account what has been accomplished and – take the fullest possible advantage of it?

*

31

Without doubt the most important advantage we can take of our human nature has to do with this power of completion through renewal.

In order to understand this we have to take account of the difference between human nature and nature in general. Whatever is natural lives and dies. Whoever is human natural lives and lives again. It cannot be put simpler than that. But

50

what are the implications of that for those of us who know and understand their human nature, faithfully and mercifully?

While we think of ourselves as natural but we have not yet discovered our human nature, as safe and sound, we experience the vicissitudes of elementary creation. This is a fancy way of saying that we are at the mercy of doubtful conditions, situations and circumstances. Our environment pushes us around and we can do nothing about it. Since we left behind the buoyancy of youth, the daily grind, it is the collective and accumulating wretchedness, misery and grief that gradually wear us down and out. We get old, even before our time, in the bad sense of the word.

From the conventional point, that is what you would expect. Running from death tires us out so much that we drop from fatigue and die. Years may pass before we discover our human nature. During those years we try to survive as best we can and it's a wonder that our human nature, prior to its discovery by us, remains available to us to the end. We all know that food and shelter sustain something but it cannot really be life because when it's time to die all the food and shelter money can buy cannot help us live longer.

This is why youth is such an important stage in our existence because while our human nature is not yet accessible as such during our youth, neither are we separated from it and merely natural. In other words during our youth we have a human natural affinity. This gives us a head start of sorts over such adults as are sunk in their immaturity, having lost their youth but not gained their human nature. Those who are privileged to teach us during our youth know of that affinity and draw on it so as to steer us in the direction of wisdom and awareness. They, like all mature adults, know of this unique principle that pertains solely to human nature, which is understood as transience and ascendance in the case of youth and as transcendence in the case of adulthood. The implication here is that when we are still young we need only to rise or pass on to our human nature but once we have left our youth and not yet gained our human nature we need to climb up to it, as it were, which takes more out of us.

In both cases, however, some experience of mere nature, of living and dying, is essential. A youth will experience this during so-called adolescence, at which time upbringing up to then counts for much. What this experience indicates to the young person is that human nature as such is something to be reckoned with, to be taken into account and that it must now be known and understood or else it will be missing and lacking. It can be called the death experience of the young. If the sum total of what adults offer to the young at this stage amounts to schemes and tactics for the acquisition of the means for the amassing of food and shelter, in other words survival values, then it can justly be said that the parental adults deliver their children to death. The young, in the face of a concerted effort of that nature, will form their own culture so as to resist as long as they may, in other words while their human natural affinity allows. From among the young will then rise those who are gifted in their desire for true human nature and this terrifies the immature adults in their vicinity.

The death experience of the young can be bitter but that of the adult is terrifying. It is as if human nature were saying to the youth: I am still with you and part of you but now you must begin to know me or taste death; while to the immature adult it says: Your being is no longer human natural and unless you begin to know me you are to all intents and purposes dead.

The immature adult can be so terrified by this that he does his utmost to deny this death experience. He will try even harder to immerse himself in the acquisition of survival values, while in the absence of human natural life he will assert his mere existence until he becomes extinct. There we must leave him for the time being.

The horror and terror of the immature adult's death experience may be mitigated and lifted temporarily out of denial and into consciousness through exposure to genuine art works. It still remains for the adult, however, to take the step then from consciousness to awareness individually and voluntarily.

The extent to which we can deny our experience of our ignorance of human nature is astonishing. Any act of transcendence in the face of the horror and the terror is therefore nothing short of heroic.

When human nature is discovered by the young, the principle of ascendance comes into play as they are wisely led and guided.

The natural desire for human nature is always a special case, which understandably arises during truly critical times. Mercy and faith are highlighted, it may even be a harsh light. Much can be accomplished at such times, over a comparatively short period of time.

*

32

What we have to look at more closely now is that act of transcendence, by an adult, in the face of adult death experience.

Confronted by mere nature, what we must come up with is the discipline of pure action and passion. The main difference between the first and all subsequent times is that at first we believe, we hope and trust, that it works while subsequently we know that it does. Understanding how and why it

works is not so important for everyone but can be very helpful for some.

Why would anyone choose the path of transcendental
discipline rather than denying, or denying yet again, the death
experience? This question cannot be answered. Also, while
we can help the young on the path with wise council, as I indicated earlier, with adults it is a case of the example being
either rejected or not. The notion that anyone can be schooled
or forced into this is absurd. Therefore the more faithful and
merciful knowledge is made available by those who know
and understand human nature the better. Knowledge of mere
nature is trivial by comparison, although so-called 'great
wonders', as we can see all too well nowadays, spring from
it. It seems all too obvious however that our frantic efforts to
increase our knowledge of mere, or non-human, nature are at
bottom misguided attempts to come to terms, in the most sophisticated fashion, with our death experience. What we gain
in this way must seem splendid on the surface but remains
limited to the sphere of survival, where we do not live again
but we merely live – and then die. Nevertheless those who
espouse their human nature may be glad that 'the time is
shortened' for them somewhat as they undertake the discipline of transcendence.

An alliance of friendship with one who undertakes this
discipline confers the benefits.

*

33

I use the term 'pure' in the present context, as in 'pure
action and passion', in comparison to 'mere', as in 'mere nature', to describe that which is motivated and guided by merciful good spirit. It would be misleading just to say: 'spiritu-
ally guided and motivated' because that would open the door

to spirit indiscriminately.) 'Mere', by comparison then, simply describes whatever is motivated or guided otherwise than by merciful good spirit.

So we do well to recognize from the very beginning that in the case of this pure action and passion, motivation and guidance come into play. Furthermore we do equally well to acknowledge that what is involved here is the motivation and guidance by merciful good spirit.

Such recognition and acknowledgement is the beginning of our discipline.

Next we could do with an explanation of what is meant by action and passion in these terms. When we act transcendentally we take our cue from this motivation and guidance and confirm in ourselves what we are beginning to know, or what we already know, of human nature and of its especial quality and value.

How does it come that we have even a notion of this special quality and value?

Action implies passion. As we confirm the motivation and guidance of merciful good spirit, we cannot help but notice how our conventional and customary qualities and values, our memories and experiences of them, will not conform to the new pattern that is emerging. This is painful. We are being motivated and guided in line with human nature even as our merely natural or survival instincts are tugging us in other directions.

The peculiar and unique pain that is involved here can be dealt with by us passionately. We give in to it. We suffer it. We do not resist, for we know that this is how it must be and that we cannot participate in our human nature while being committed to the merely natural system of causes and events. The pain indicates to us the actual effectiveness of our commitment to human nature but it also shows us how we still cling to survival values and how we are still mixed up in them.

The most important understanding for us is, that the purely voluntary suffering of this pain helps to set us free from those merely natural patterns of existence. Intelligently we appreciate that those bad habits of ours do not cause pain but that the urge and willingness to replace them with good, human natural habits is attended by this merely natural reaction of pain, so that is suffices for us passionately to 'let go'.

We do not turn away from our participatory action in order to deal with the pain separately. This again would be misguided. Transcending action and passion are one. It's up to us to know this and to remember it at the appropriate time. Just as the action, if it were pursued in denial of the pain and short of passion, would no longer be transcendent but transgressive, so would passion heedless of action no longer serve but disturb and undermine. The transcendent action is also passionate. The transcendent passion is also active.

*

34

It is our self that militates against transcendence. It is our self or ego that strengthens itself by resisting the death and destruction of mere nature. It would have us believe that unless we resist, we will ourselves die and be destroyed. As soon as we believe that, our death and destruction commence. It is also our ego or self that urges us to ignore the efficacy of suffering pain and to trespass passionless into some realm of the supernatural. However this realm of the supernatural literally impersonates our human nature. It stands for an effete spirituality, devoid of faith and mercy. It also manages to frighten us into submission because its advocates, in whatever guise, actually celebrate their lack of humanity.

So we can see that between self-assertion and self-sacrifice there is not much to choose. Vehement self-assertion really has nothing to do with passion, which implies a glad suffering and therefore dissolution of the pain caused by our resistance of the urge to be human-natural. We might describe someone as 'falling into a passion'. This clearly implies a separating-out of heated feelings, away from any true action. Such a separation is never possible in the case of transcendence, where action and passion are one.

Just as we may fly into merely natural passion<u>s</u> (motion<u>s</u>, feeling<u>s</u> etc.) we may also stray into merely natural actions. Another word for merely natural action, empty of compassion, is demonic action. Merely natural passion, compared to this, is morbid. We may observe the triumphant demon and the morbid victim. Both are to be pitied because of their lack of human nature. They do not transcend their mere nature but they testify incidentally to their need to do so. If we try to help them we fortify our own human nature. If we show the demonic individual human natural compassion, which is informed by our particular pity for him in his state, he is brought closer to an insight into the beauty of human nature. Thereby he is not judged, criticized or condemned for having strayed into the realm of the supernatural but he is shown the example of an alternative that is human and not demonic. Similarly, if we demonstrate for the morbid individual an example of human natural activity he may be moved to forego the pleasure of his merely natural attachments in favour of something worthwhile.

I can recall, with distinct gratitude, incidents in my own past existence when I was able to benefit from someone's human natural compassion after having strayed into the realm of the demonic, or when, after having slid into morbidity, the effectiveness of human natural activity was demonstrated for me. I also know now that those who did me such a service were not left unrewarded.

*

35

The discipline of pure action and passion can be described as co-operative with merciful good spirit. At the same time it is important for us to accept that *we* may be at fault while our human nature is safe and sound. Next we need to know that we do not need to wait until we are constricted by some death, or as some call it: near-death, experience before we can actively and passionately transcend from merely natural being to human natural being. We want to be capable of communality, that is our chief aim and we want to get away from any Social compulsions, from doing, thinking and feeling in ways that are motivated by the desire to be popular, to be liked, to seek safety in numbers, to reject the truth and prefer falsehood, to uphold standards for the purpose of superiority over other beings, and so on. Every individual, as he sets out on this path of discipline, has his particular Social hang-ups pointed out to him by the pain, the discomfort and inconvenience that arises for him. If someone else were to describe such a discipline to him, he would automatically come up with arguments to the contrary that would testify to the various aspects of his make-up where in the past he has allowed himself to become committed to merely natural survival values. No, he needs no one else to point the finger. He has to figure it out for himself from those above-mentioned indicators.

Of course someone without the basic human affinity who is not even conscious in himself of any communal urge or of any experience of death will simply laugh. That lets the one who has inadvertently described the path of discipline to him know that his description has been accurate.

It can also happen that someone tries to cheat, by pretending to a communality which he does not have, but that becomes laughable then for those who are in possession of the genuine article.

Most important of all is the understanding that we are not our nature, that I and my nature are not the same. Think of it as a fact that your nature is safe and sound and that frequently you yourself seem to be faulty and at risk. It's no use pretending that you yourself are all right most of the time except when you slip up and then you have to discover some flaw in your character or something remiss in your personality. Instead turn and return to your nature. Make sure however that it's your human nature. If it flatters you or condemns you, you are on the wrong track. If it makes you feel forceful or undermines your watchfulness or attentiveness you are also on the wrong track.

Know therefore that the sign you are looking for is total peace. Discard all other signs. Ignore them and keep searching. You may have to put some effort into it but never to the exclusion of common sense. Let no sensation or idea put you off course. Total peace is not a feeling. If you have this wonderful feeling of peace, that is something else. Don't stop with that. Issue a pleasant greeting and pass on. Don't look inside or outside yourself. Your human nature and total peace are not there.

Here is another thing: There is not necessarily any call for you to stop doing whatever else you might be doing. However if you cannot pay heed or attend to your human nature without stopping what you are doing, then you should stop because you must be doing something that is detrimental to you as a human being. If you continue nevertheless with that activity or passivity you will definitely do yourself harm, although you may not know what sort of harm, or not until later.

36

Your human nature announces itself as a great peace. As a result, much that has wormed its way into the domain of your high regard, to lay claim to your respect and admiration, will fade from view like a ghost at dawn.

However I would strongly urge you to continue to know what is going on. This is not the time for lying back to let the sun shine up your nostrils. I say it merely to put it on record. You are under surveillance now, having been entrusted. That exemplary immolation of your self is a thing of the past now and the only selfishness you will know in future will be passed on to you so that you may correspond to it, in peaceful fashion. You will, as I say, have to keep your eyes open because your peace attracts customers but if you get lazy it attracts flies.

Do, however, enjoy this total peace. Do compare it to the attractions of Society now and again and whether you find yourself on cushions or in a field you will smile and say: There is no comparison. In a cell at her majesty's pleasure or as keeper of the household keys you will smile and say: Truly, there is no comparison.

Ever so much will be going on meanwhile, within you and elsewhere on your behalf, so you might as well believe that and draw comfort from it. Coincidences will be pointers. Soon you will be on nodding acquaintance with the unforeseeable. Keep your shoes laced up tight if you own a pair because suddenly it will be time to walk a mile or ten. Also, don't mind being invisible. In those days they will walk right through you without noticing. If you wait for apologies, time will hang heavy on your hands. Don't be in a rush to link up with kindred spirits. In time, *they* will find *you*.

And always keep in mind that however you fare, all is for the best.

*

37

Total peace is you in the possession of your human nature. After a while you get the hang of it. You will say to yourself: Is it worthwhile doing anything else now except to enjoy this peace? Have I not been ever so busy for ever so long running away from my self as my enemy, thereby colluding with that enemy? Now let me finally take my ease among those who have probably known all along what it is all about but they were too polite to set me straight.

Naturally you are apt to experiment with this peace. How far will it stretch? What all will it cover? How long does it last? When they call you a dropout, or lazy, or irresponsible, can you peacefully cope with that or do you get furious?

One thing is sure, you cannot keep doing things for the same reasons. Many of your reasons in the past seem now after all to have been spurious. They were manufactured after the act to justify your self. Your devious self was rarely at a loss when it came to pursuing its goals and covering its tracks. Now it seems to make sense to wait until you can behave spontaneously.

But you are looking at the world through new eyes. At times you are curiously reminded of how the world appeared to you when you were a child. Scenes from childhood recur memorably. And you like to spend time by yourself. There is no shortage at all of things to think about quietly, especially since these things come to you cloaked in gratitude. They are grateful to you for thinking about them. Besides, thinking now is more like a contemplative pastime than an intellectual exercise. Your thinking no longer goes on compulsively or obsessively, driven by anxiety and in some compartment separate from feeling. Your attitude is whole. You have come into your inheritance: that seems to be a very suitable description of it.

*

38

The most shocking thing for you to face during this initial enjoyment of total peace, of your human nature in its totality, is self-interest in someone else. In the possession of your human nature you, like it, are safe and sound and you cannot for the life of you imagine at this stage why anyone would take trouble and go to any length to establish and secure himself, when this security all so obviously (to you) and entirely depends on one's human nature as it is evidently (for you) available nowadays. Surely, you suppose, if *you* can attain to it so can anyone! And yet where you look now you see a hustle and bustle and a thousand attempts in the dark to catch phantoms while the reality in the light, in the open (where you are) makes no demands on its own behalf and constricts no souls for the wanting of it.

I say it is a shocking thing because you cannot imagine yourself in the company of such people for any length of time without seriously falling out with them. This may cast a grave shadow over your existence. On one hand you have the total peace that dissolves all problems while on the other hand your longing to persevere in this peace in the company of others is thwarted at every turn.

The most commonsensical policy would seem to be to avoid people altogether. You don't need them, do you? Let them build their sand castles, create their wealth and fight their wars; let them squabble over who gets the dead granny's house, who becomes the director of the company, who is the first to discover a quark and to secure the patent for his efforts. It all seems so futile, so puerile!

Over all this do you perhaps tend to forget what it was that motivated your search in the first place, namely the desire really and truly to communicate, to enter into communal relationship with beings and to leave behind the isolation and separation implied by society? Will it dawn on you eventually that the total peace you have gained is not so much an end in itself as the fluid context and contingency for creative action and passion? You do understand what it means to be creative. You do not so much do what you feel like doing and what you like to do but you love to overcome your dislikes and antipathies. These people, when you notice how they behave once they get wind of how much you enjoy your total peace – do you not dislike them and find them antipathetic? They are envious. You show them contempt. They are jealous. You hate them for it. Something is definitely wrong here.

*

39

It's not surprising, on the surface, that troubled people in the presence of someone totally at peace can tell that something they need is more available than usual. However if that person is not offering his peace but so to speak hoarding it for himself they will 'persecute'. They will not know or admit that this is what they are doing but they will in fact persecute that person in one way or another. I am talking specifically about troubled people here, not about some wise man who knows when a person is hoarding his peace and can therefore advise him to offer it instead.

The psychology of persecution has to unmask the persecution, for the benefit of the one who would be better off not persecuting, but that same psychology must then also reveal to the one who hoards his peace that he does so. What concerns us at the moment is the latter of those two options. If you feel you are being persecuted, what should you do? According to our present reading of the situation it would be in your best interests to make your peace with it and extend it to those who are giving you bother. That is not the same as 'taking the blame on yourself. It is simply being practical in the most expedient way. Of course you won't feel like doing this. You have to take the trouble to think about it and to call something to mind that you understand, something you have previously bothered to understand, as you might in fact be doing now. I, as I write this, refresh my mind about it. I recall incidents when I neglected to do what I advocate here and I recall also how much trouble and bother it caused me, which was unnecessary. This makes me feel stupid and contrite, which is also helpful. We all hate hypocrisy.

How can we extend or offer our peace to someone, that is really the burning issue here. Once we get into the habit it becomes the most natural, that is to say human natural, behaviour in the world, however to the extent that we have the bad habit of clinging to our peace as though it could be cornered we have to take pains to think things through. While we are being pestered or nagged at, this is not the best time for sorting things out, because then we merely react, fearfully or aggressively. Perhaps it should also be mentioned that we are dealing with a very particular kind of persecution here, not with racial persecution, on account of skin colour or country of origin, nor with tribal persecutions, such as adherents to different religions inflict on each other. In such cases no total peace is available, for the lack of human nature and communality. Advocacy of contumely is after all standard Social behaviour. We hate Christians, Jews, Arabs, whites, blacks, Serbs, Bosnians, communists, capitalists because they threaten our Social identity which is, I suppose, based upon a kind of peace such as we get from self-complacency and from the vanity based on sheer superiority of numbers.

If you have total peace and you know you do, why not take the time to express it? If ever expression was invented to serve a purpose, this surely is it. How you express it is up to you and no one else can choose a form for you. Think of it as the cusp of your genuine personality and your personality must be powered by your unique and singular individuality, not by considerations of popularity, which would be Social.

An expression of peace makes peace available to others.

*

40

It may seem like a peculiar thought but the fact is that your expressing of peace, of the peace we mean here, protects you against invasion. You will no doubt be familiar by now with the invasive forces that smite you as you travel among those who say they love you and those who don't. For one thing, as you express your peace, this gives you something to do, so you don't sit around in anxiety waiting to be persecuted. This will be less likely, now that you no longer hug your salvation to yourself.

I despair of being able to explain what I mean by the expression of peace to anyone without the human natural taste for communality. Our concern for the young is one thing. There everything is possible. However, once a man has set his heart against the power of renewal and daily takes infinite care, as it were, to close his mind tightly in case a merciful notion should enter, we must leave him to his chosen category and consider instead the welfare of the one who is open to good spirit but perplexed no end by the varied influences and manifold effects of a love that is all too often more readily misapprehended than appreciated.

Inasmuch as you have identified some peaceful sensation within yourself and you suppose you want it inside, all for yourself and perhaps for some God or idol that has meanwhile cropped up to claim your attention, this is where you may initiate an outward impulse, again in one form or another, to be decided upon by yourself. My own form at present is written language. It could as readily be spoken language. Of course you have to give up that sensation but that is by the by. What you must confirm, thanks to what you have learned, is that the peace that would solve all your problems has an outward dimension to it. It is whole and will not, can not, be constrained inwardly. It is intolerant of exclusivity. What you do therefore when you express it is prove to yourself just that. At the same time you reveal it to others. All those 'others' – you have become so afraid of them perhaps in the meanwhile! In reality they are not a danger to *you* but to your morbid preconceptions. You try to hide your peace inside and that makes you fair game. Look at it this way. Within yourself and without yourself come together to make a whole. The human natural peace is whole. Let a sensation of it tempt you to possessiveness rather than persuade you to expression and instead of that potentially fruitful inward domain a sickening of your inside takes place. The 'inside' replaces the inward. Melancholy sets in. Hypochondria. A morose spirit curls its tentacles around your human nature and would draw it into the depth. Here we have the cause of all sickness. You no longer espouse the soundness of human nature, so what can you expect? You take a thousand risks because you ignore its safety. A thousand industries exist, more than eager to deal with you on terms that are half-hearted. In that way sickness becomes the norm and possessiveness the standard.

*

This total peace, which links our human nature and communality, is not given to us so that we sit down with it while twiddling our thumbs. Sensations of it do occur, not so that we may swoon with self-appreciation and indulge in contempt for those who are troubled but so that we will even at this late date interpret our state and express our peace. There is no need to wait for a sensation of it but if one comes let it betoken an emergency.

Whether we know of our peace through emergent sensation or intuitively, the decision to make it available for others is based on understanding. It is based on our understanding not of the peace but of its purpose, its reason for occurring to us. The purpose is communication. The reason is community.

Can we make communication and community happen by expressing our peace? Not at all. What we can do in this way is set the example. What we may take note of then is who follows the example and who does not.

What we are setting is a personal example of peace. There will be those who rise to the occasion in the face of such an example. This implies communication. If I rise to the occasion of your personal example of peace, expressed by you in one way or another, I participate with you in communication. This is what it means to communicate. The peace is like the bridge across which we agree to meet halfway. However the act of communication is always spontaneous. It's absurd to call someone a bad communicator. He may be a bad entertainer, but communication is a free response to total peace. It cannot be calculated, practiced or prepared for. I can say that communication between you and me is at present not coming about but if I want it to come about I must see to my expression of my peace, to the example I am setting and do my best there, not criticize your personality or perhaps your attention span. I must do my best, and that means also that it makes no sense for me to blame myself if no communication succeeds because no one can make it happen. It is not in anyone's hands to make communication happen.

On the other hand, if I do not rise to the occasion of *your* example of expressed total peace, I become harder hearted and stiffer necked and narrower minded, that sort of thing, which no one looks forward to. I do well, therefore to look forward to the next time when I might be able to rise to an occasion of total peace.

There is the one who expresses the peace and there is the one who does or does not rise to the occasion of it. There is community or society. There is communication or – entertainment?

*

42

Which brings us around nicely to the main part of our topic, which is society. So far we have only skirted the fringes of it, by having a look at Society, whereupon we sheared away from that towards community and communication.

As soon as community appears on the scene, so does society. The advent of total peace, and of course its exemplary expression, makes that obvious. If you are not entering into communication with me – and it cannot be up to me to decide whether you are unable or unwilling – then our concourse and discourse will be social.

This is indeed what 'happens' now. It happens rather than being done. In addition, it will continue to happen while one of us expresses total peace, being totally peaceful, and the other one does not rise to the occasion.

What I mean by society here is really a most peculiar state of affairs and it has to be looked at from various angles if we hope to do it justice.

For the sake of understanding and in the hope of not rubbing anyone up the wrong way I am going to speak of the peaceful person and the popular individual. Let me introduce a purely scientific note. Popular individuals among themselves cannot come up with society, but they can socialize (Socialize?), which is productive of Society and carefully avoided by any peaceful person so far as lies in his or her power. Peaceful persons, on the other hand, have community in common and they communicate, while popular individuals at best look on.

When we look at society, things become a bit more complicated and we will have to decide, as we get on, how much of the complication is due to our looking at it and studying it and how much of it can be simplified for the purpose of practical existence.

We know that people have it in them to be human and that human beings are liable to become popular. We know this but I suppose we should never tire of repeating it at crucial moments. Human beings are eager to do good. People smile when you say that. They know all about these do-gooders, and so on. But let's not be scornful. Once a human being has wrung himself through to a mature experience of total peace and once he has learned how to express that peace, he will want to know what is best for him to do in the company of those who reject his peace or simply do not take it up. He will still want to do good but it will be more a case of him doing his best. He will continue to express his peace but the expression will take on a form. It will take on a suitable form. He still has the same goods on offer but now its as if he were bringing them to the market or to the negotiating table. What he says, what he does and how he behaves will automatically be fashioned to best suit the popular individual's, or individuals', present state of being. He cannot be polite, since politeness is a Social manner but he will know how not to be impolite – by being civil. He cannot be kind, since kindness is a Social manner but he will know how not to be unkind – by being kindly.

So far it looks like the peaceful person, when confronted by Society, is faced mainly with the task of making allowances. It looks on the surface as if instead of doing something he is more concerned about what not to do. Let's not forget, however, that he is still laying his peace on the line, in terms of civility and kindliness, and he has not formed a judgement as to the worthiness of anyone. He is creatively occupied, especially now that he has to overcome an assortment of disappointments and frustrations in himself in view of the rejection or ignorance he comes up against. He has his hands almost full just keeping in mind that it is not he himself who is being ignored or rejected but his natural humanity, his communality and his total peace.

*

43

There is a passage in one or two of the 'Gospels', as they are called, that refers to a man letting his peace go out to the worthy and letting it return to him in company of the unworthy. What I mean when I describe our human approach to others seems to me to be just that. A kind of clever adjustment is certainly required, based upon an awareness, I suppose, of our state of peace. It does not always return to us automatically when a fool, who has said in his heart there is no good, leaves us gasping for air. We require at such moments the spur of learning, of having been taught how to help ourselves, lest we go under rather than undergoing.

This, then, is how far a true man (or woman, to be sure) behaves socially and it circumscribes the extent to which he makes allowances for society. Has he a duty to society? He has indeed, but we must keep the meaning of the word society clear in our consciences. Unless we take it to connote a thing that is half done and half comes about we lose ourselves on the wrong road. Are we safe to think of it as other than a narrow path, sometimes along the cliff edge and when we kick off a stone it rolls so far that we stop, astonished?

The popular individual knows nothing of society. He is Social. I myself am Social when I concern myself more over who likes me than over those I love.

It appears that what I need around me, if what I get is anything to go by, is the casual companionship of a few who have not yet made up their minds, who stand in a state of flux between individualism and communality. I believe that what attracts them to me is that I neither condemn their uncertainties nor withhold from them what I believe to be worth believing. I do not dress my opinion as dogma but I disguise my certainties as opinions. My society is a courtesy I extend to those few, inasmuch as we are all of us fallible, whether we just confess it or not. If suddenly I perceive a glimmer of the light of day through the pedestrian daylight, I am overjoyed and grateful and more than ready to lay aside the cautions of my society for the purpose of community.

Only rarely am I able to choose my company. It is given to me. I am placed where I exist and I trust this is good, if not at least better than preferences I might construe from imagined pleasure elsewhere. Acquaintances come and go. Here is one who hangs on me, who surrounds me with attentions, with invitations, and offers me a type of warmth I detest. Nevertheless I extend to him the social courtesy (the form) that occurs to me at the moment. It is not a set pattern or pre-

71

scribed recipe but rather a handling and dealing from point to point, a chopping and changing as my esteem falls or my gorge rises. There will be – I know that because it is one of my certainties – a satisfactory outcome of one sort or another because I am never kept long under such a duress, even though I consider the cheerful endurance of it as an aspect of my appointed task on terra firma.

Here comes another, who embodies the worst derelictions of the discarded misfit. I am drawn to him because I sense in him an anxiety for beneficial change. Having long laid aside, as much as I could tell, all Social principles, I overlook the alcoholism, the drug addiction, the penchant to prevarication if not outright lying, the filthy rags and filthier language and concentrate my attentiveness on what rightly or wrongly I perceive as a genuine grief. On that I build my communal hopes. Communal expectations I limit. All social anticipations I cast to the wind. I might go so far as to proffer a clean pair of trousers and I may insist that my house remain alcohol- and cocaine-free but as to any permanent conversion to sound sense and sobriety, I have learned through hard experience to leave that to powers greater than I can muster. I can pray that a man might see sense, as indeed I do for myself, but I cannot set him upon such a thing as some call the 'right path'.

*

44

From the point of view then of the one who is practiced in communal being and doing, society is an intermediary and temporary relation between himself and those who are not committed to Society but neither have they espoused yet their communal prerogative. What he is bound to reject is any and all Social overtures or urges. His intentions is to communicate, in truth. He does not prejudge anyone in order to estimate their communicability but he expresses his peace and

thereupon the next step is revealed to him. If his peace "re-
turns to him", to borrow that phrase, he simply says yes to
that. It means for him that at present there is nothing to be
done; that no community, no society, only Society is possible. A struggle may ensue within himself. Perhaps some
weakness in himself for being Social is being revealed to
him. This can always happen again. He will feel equally inclined to indulge and to reject. That is the character of the
struggle. He will want to end that struggle, to step out of it, as
soon as possible. Neither the rejection nor the indulgence lies
open to him. He has only the one option and that is to express
his peace more assertively. As he expresses it, so he experiences it then – inasmuch as it is not being accepted.

This could be called the chief social act – to be courte-
ous nevertheless – because of its decisive nature. It ends the
struggle so that he has neither to indulge nor to reject the Social being. He would be equally compromised in both cases.

It would be entirely futile to prescribe particular rules
and regulations for this social act. The question: How shall I
express my peace in the event of such a struggle in myself? –
can only be answered by: It will be given to you to know at
the time. But of course you have to be alert at the time to the
implications of the event and to your giftedness as a mature
human being.

It must be obvious that such an asserted expression of
peace is creative. We cannot feel like doing it; our body is
never inclined to lend itself to assertiveness. We cannot do it
in reliance on precedent; our mind is faced every such time
with something new in itself. It is therefore I myself, you
yourself, who must personally step into the breach, in our
habit of peace. It does become a good habit if it is not yet
one. It can never be routine.

*

45

The struggle, the 'socialist' struggle, as I am going to call it for a while, is worth examining in detail. The mature person, the communal being, is bound to reject any Social overture, wherever and however it approaches him. This description of 'being bound' hints at the constraint involved. It is a most complicated state to be in. At the same time he cannot help but indulge in the Social impulsion, which therefore becomes compulsive. Although he is bound to reject, he cannot and although he cannot help but indulge, he may not.

An analysis of the socialist struggle would be pointless. Only two things are really of interest and that is first of all the timely recognition of it and then our assertion of our total peace. An analysis of that assertion could be profitable but the motivation for it would have to be handled with kid gloves. We do not assert our peace in the face of the socialist struggle so as to be rid of an annoyance nor do we do so in order to triumph over an enemy. Any motivation for such an assertion of total peace cannot lie outside or beyond or previous to that peace as we know it.

I think it may not be so inappropriate after all to describe this struggle as socialist because the real temptation after all does exit, for the peaceful person, do 'make a thing' out of the social experience, that is to say not to see it and understand it as intermediary and temporary but as something in itself and final which can, as a relation, be forced, manipulated and controlled. I am fully aware, by the way, of the wider implications of all this. Meanwhile it does hit the mark to characterize the effect of the struggle itself on the mature, communal and peaceful person as a temptation. He is not tempted to reject the Social approach, he is <u>bound</u> to reject it. Likewise he is not tempted to indulge in it but he <u>cannot help</u> but indulge in it. What does tempt him is the struggle as such.

He almost feels obliged to throw himself into the fray. The nature of the struggle that tempts him is the same whether he is involved with just one individual, with several or with many. He seems to see an opportunity for flexing his muscles. Energy is on the go and why should he not have some for himself? Indeed there is a whiff of 'power' in the air. It's only political, but it's power. Political power is not the ability to do good but the ability to change the world and that is a vastly different kettle of fish.

*

46

We may imagine, again, the peaceful human being on one side and the popular individual on the other. There is a confrontation of the Social element and the communal substance. The human being begins to struggle, he finds himself involved in a struggle, inasmuch as he is bound to reject the Social overture and because he cannot help but indulge in it. He is at once challenged and seduced. This is what he suddenly enough finds on his plate, or in his in-tray, to deal with. He is tempted to behave in terms of that struggle, to act on the basis of his findings, to reject judiciously what he feels like rejecting and to indulge languidly what in his opinion is pleasurable.

We have to be quite clear about the fact that so far he has not committed or compromised himself. Being tempted, he does not yet give in to the temptation. His involvement in the struggle is not voluntary but accidental. The very first time it is even unavoidable. It is quite possible for him to see clearly what is going on, even though what is going on is painful, disturbing and very likely exciting. He may not be in favour of what he sees but he cannot plead ignorance since his vision is mature and gifted. Also, because he does see clearly, he cannot dispute the fact that he is at present involved in something foreign to his human nature. How this happened may be a puzzle to him. That it has happened is undeniable. That he might have prevented it from happening, this is the source of a nagging doubt, of a questionable guilt, of a distinct sorrow. That it may after all be a good thing, a fortuitous event, this is the exciting part, the hopeful sensation, the promise of vitality – the delusion.

At this stage, prior to any giving in to the temptation of voluntary, intentional involvement by him, we can, I believe, speak of the struggle as socialist. It means that we recognize the risk to potential social action by the mature person, the danger of a short-circuiting of society that would be caused by the Social element in combination with the complicity of the human being, who would thereby of course slip into immaturity.

We do well to keep in mind throughout all this that the so-called Social element is actually espoused by the popular individual. He is not himself that element, nor is he an innocent at the mercy of destructive forces. Neither is the peaceful human being the gift of communality but he accepts that gift in terms of his majority and is of course at liberty to neglect the investment of it. So just as we cannot plead the innocence of ignorance if we are Social and motivated by popularity, so we cannot pretend to the superiority of being infallible if we are communal and human natural. We may think of ourselves as the salt of the earth but if we do not accept the struggle that is being described here and the creative confrontation of it as an important aspect of our task of work, the salt loses its savour.

*

47

We have come to the point now where the actual, voluntary and intentional involvement, no matter how begrudging or enthusiastic, of the peaceful human being in the socialist struggle has to be contemplated.

Having become involved in the tempting socialist struggle, this has of course put paid for the time being to his enjoyment of total peace. The fact that he could not have counted on this, at least not at that particular time, that is part of the struggle. It is after all the root of that combination of regret and excitement. However he is still a peaceful human being inasmuch as he may express his peace. The expression of it, being a passionately creative act, does not depend on any sensation he has of it but solely on his certainty of belief that he possesses it – that he is endowed with it.

What we are contemplating here then is the attempt to rid oneself of the struggle and to achieve peace by coming down on the side of indulgence or on the side of rejection. However because of the peculiar nature of the case, neither of these is a workable option for us, as was indicated earlier and this is soon enough pointed out to us. The indulgence turns sour, the rejection becomes problematic; the struggle, instead of fading, becomes more intense.

Our next attempt at an achievement of the peace which cannot be achieved could be described as power-brokering, more accurately as behaviour based on the wish that contradictory forces might be balanced, played off against each other. In short, we come up with policies. We take part now in the struggle. We behave immaturely. It begins to look different to us now, this conflict of interests, this ongoing dispute over punishments and rewards, this mixture of cravings for justice without humility, for rights without responsibility and privilege without duty. We have our hands full, it's a wearying business but we do have our eye on the success of peace, eventually restored. However total peace cannot be restored. All that can be restored is a temporary suspension of hostilities, a short-lived pacification of riotous elements, a momentary appeasement of belligerent wills.

The struggle can now be described as political.

*

48

The peaceful human being, as we have defined him, knows what it means to enjoy total peace, we can be sure of that. It is therefore onerous for him suddenly to find himself struggling. Someone who has never tasted such peace may be involved in a struggle of one sort or another for years. Not having total peace to compare it to, he views it differently. But then the struggle which is socialist in nature is unique because it is after all being experienced by someone who has known total or whole peace.

As soon as we sense that this struggle is upon us we can express our peace and there's an end to it. That is of course the simplest solution. The more schooled we are in our peace the more sensitively are we ready for even the very beginnings of this struggle in ourselves and the quicker are we off the mark when it comes to expressing our peace. At first we resent being troubled. Total peace is a central experience. Small wonder that after the first time we suppose we are fixed for life. And of course we are, but we need to be tempted and tested, otherwise will we not rest on our laurels? The social action I am describing not only makes total peace available to others but it also strengthens us in our growth. The communal action springs directly from our giftedness. In it we are not troubled and there is no struggle. The creation is spontaneous and free. The social action by comparison can be seen as effectively feeding into it. This is another reason why we should not shy away from facing the Social element head on whenever it challenges or seduces us. This is not the same as toying with it or seeking it out. Since it has no face of its own, simply facing it is enough to outface it, but we can only face it peacefully. Our face is our peace.

*

49

What it takes, when the time comes for us to face up to the struggle, is valor. This is the chief social virtue. It has to be learned through hard experience. It refers to the strength we gain and to the strength we need when facing up to the socialist struggle.

Remember that the socialist struggle, as I use the word 'socialist', is not political. It does not become political until we have, in cowardly fashion, discovered that rejection and indulgence both only make things worse and then we participate in the struggle. This could be called cowardice in action.

The valorous action, which is essentially an expression of peace while under the duress of the socialist struggle, has this particular detailed effect, that it draws to our attention and to the attention of those who have eyes to see, that which is valid and has value and that which has none and is worthless. It draws this to our attention. It differentiates between the two. No criticism, judgement or condemnation is involved. When we say: This is a sound potato and this is a rotten potato, we simply describe. The value comes into it as soon as we have decided that we want to do something with the potatoes. If we want to eat them, the sound one is valid and the rotten one worthless. If we want to add to the garden compost, the rotten one has the value.

So value is tied to use, to employment and application.

Transfer this now to our discussion of society. What use do we have for those with whom we come into association? If we have no use for them, nothing in mind for them that will

79

make them useful for us, then we have become indifferent participants in the socialist struggle. In fact, having no use for those around us is the quickest way to slide into indulgence or rejection, which is the preliminary stage of the cowardly regression, from which we pass on then, unless we express our peace, to the political struggle, where not value counts but policy. The energy we invest in this political struggle automatically confers a political use on those around us, to the extent that they fit into, or correspond to, a policy of ours. So political use, which adheres to policy, is something vastly different from peaceful use, which confers value.

Criticism, judgement and condemnation are an aspect of the political struggle. When we feel like criticizing or condemning we are involved in that struggle and being tempted to act in cowardly fashion. An expression of peace, an act of valor, will overrule that inclination and show us, perhaps again, whether someone can be of peaceful use to us or not.

By peaceful use I mean everything that is implied by fellowship in community and friendship in person.

A political ally can be trusted while he agrees with our policy. A friend is useful to us because we trust him. There is cowardly trust and valorous trust.

*

50

Let's assume now that we find ourselves struggling in some association and that we have decided to express our peace rather than get involved in the struggle or even participate in it politically. Let's assume we have decided to make a valorous move. As we express our peace, what we want to know is whether or not those we have to do with can be of use in terms of community and friendship. All we have to go on initially is the accidental experience of struggle, which may comprise anything from fondness and the most enthusiastic partiality to mistrust, distaste and downright loathing.

The peace we express guards us from the start against prejudice we would otherwise automatically come up with. In the absence of that expression we would, in the conventional idiom, 'fall for' or 'fall out with' the individual or individuals we have to do with. So favourable or unfavourable bias is ruled out. On reflection we know how silly it would be to pretend to any real knowledge or appreciation, any so-called objective appraisal on the basis or in terms of that initial problematic state which testifies after all to a great mixture of ingredients, such as what we ourselves amount to at that moment, our constitution, mood and temperament just then, our state of mind and emotion and how all this comes together with the complex state of being of the one we have met. Had we met under different circumstances I might not have experienced distaste at all, or attraction, or boredom. If someone other than myself had met you he might have liked you right away or found you a little perverse.

So all those initial experiences we have of each other, or of one another if more than two are party to the meeting, are not valid. They have no value. They may be pleasant or unpleasant, flattering of off-putting, but what they all equally are is useless. Community and friendship cannot grow from them and it would be a pity if they were prevented by them.

The groundbreaking social act, then, is a peaceful inquiry as to the possibility of community or friendship. It is a courageous or valorous act because we overcome our inclination to indulge or reject. We don't ever feel like making that sort of inquiry. What we feel like is favouring or condemning.

Certainly any response to your observant openness, to your attentive receptivity, will never reflect on anyone's character, qualities or potential. Neither will it let you know that this person is worth or not worth knowing, nor will it tell you anything about your own capacity for relationship. It does however enlighten you as to the possibility or lack of possibility of relationship, of fellowship, of association to begin with. If even so much as an association comes about, this is of value. Association is useful. It does not partake of community or friendship but it counts as a victory in the face of Society and as positive gain in comparison to anything you might have based on an 'evaluation' or judgement of anyone.

Association, although it is a beginning of sorts, is still troublesome and problematic. A further expression of peace is required to decide the matter. It is quite possible to get stuck in association, to lose any ground gained.

*

51

We can describe the beginnings of social intercourse as association and as peaceful inquiry into the possibility of community or friendship. As soon as we speak of intercourse however we presuppose mutual commitment; we stand back and pronounce upon processes and exchanges for which we cannot vouch ingenuously. This opens the door to hypocrisy, even professional hypocrisy; perhaps especially professional hypocrisy.

Therefore, for the time being at least, I intend to disregard the possibility of any genuine knowledge of such a thing as social intercourse and concentrate instead on what I, or anyone else for that matter, can vouch for and that is the presence or absence in ourselves of any predisposition to that peaceful inquiry. I can create that predisposition and am therefore responsible for it. If I do not create it I am guilty of neglect or oversight. Guilt, as a psychic sensation now, informs me as to such a shortfall in my responsible creativity, whereupon I can put matters right regretfully.

This creative, or created, predisposition of myself, or in your case of yourself, to the peaceful inquiry is and remains entirely individual and not at all personal. What we do here we do in secret. No one else knows about it, and we do not speak of god as of someone else. Without question we have our hands full usually because at the best of times the Social challenges are numerous. The more sensitive we become to such challenges, the more refined our knowledge becomes of the various implications and possible consequences, the more do we also strive to understand more charitably those we come into contact with. However this also means that we are able to deal with more intense and more numerous challenges. The onus is on us therefore to make a good habit of peaceful enquiry without waiting for such challenges. This means nothing more or less than cultivating a lively interest in those around us for the express purpose of community and friendship.

Pathological cravings for community and friendship are not possible. Whatever we pathologically crave is Socially determined. It speaks for our unwillingness to express our peace – but equally does it testify to our capacity for expressing it. It may be bad news but more important is its aspect as good news. The healer is always much more aware of the good news aspect. He may see quite clearly the penchant for a 'folie a deux' or a 'folie a plusieurs' for that matter but his therapeutic agency will be enlisted in terms of the implied capacity for friendship or community, even though it has gone wrong.

I would call it the habit of fellowship, which we acquire when we cultivate a lively interest in those around us for the express purpose of friendship and community. Individually and in secret we continue to be just as alert and alive to any Social challenges, just as quick to predispose ourselves again and again to the expression of our total peace, and to inward inquiry as to the possibility of community and friendship, but now a personal dimension is added.

Within the context of what we mean by society this can only amount to a dimension. Until now we have been inwardly active and passive and outwardly only passive. When it comes to fellowship we allow for a degree of outward activity. Wisdom is required and the more experience the better.

Remember we are discussing and working out something specific here. The habit of fellowship is social, neither Social nor communal. Our human nature is involved but not laid on the line. Why would anyone cultivate such a habit? For two reasons, I suppose. One, in order to pre-empt as many Social challenges as possible and two, to become more effective and therefore stronger as a human being. They are of course functions of one and the same habit. Like all good habits, once fully acquired, fellowship becomes spontaneous.

*

52

The cultivation of fellowship, is a personal activity in the social realm. Only mature human beings are capable of it because only they are able to keep in mind simultaneously the eventuality of a Social challenge culminating in a socialist struggle and the possibility of community and friendship in response to an expression of total peace.

Meanwhile we should keep in mind that fellowship, as I use the word here, is not an end in itself like community or friendship. Being social, it is intermediate. It is 'meanwhile', for the time being. There is no steadiness of purpose to it. It is not a settled state. Personal activity however does come into it, and of a very particular kind.

The best way to describe it might be in terms of a confession of faith. This sounds simple enough except that what is required is not what is conventionally called a religious faith but something quite different, which I have always in the past referred to as human natural faith.

Those who have not become too sickened by the prevailing hypocrisy to ever wish to use the word god might be able to accept that such human natural faith is in fact a being in god. If we say that we have this faith in god we mean nothing more than that. It is not a faith that can be attached to this or that entity or object. We cannot have human natural faith in our selves or in one another or in the airbus that is transporting us to another country. We can only have it in god, but to say that is almost a pleonasm because to have it means to have it in god inasmuch as it means to be in god.

Now we know that as mature human beings we are alive to our human nature. That means that human natural faith is something we automatically have. We do not first have to acquire it. We can of course be more or less alive to it and any demonstration we give of that ability can be called a confession of human natural faith or an act of fellowship.

*

53

We can see now that within the social context our individual expression of total peace culminates in personal confessions of human natural faith.

Being alive and alert to our human nature we are able to see clearly in those around us their existential pain, by which I mean their lack of connectedness to their human nature. We do not however see this in separation from our own human nature, from an analytical distance or as though we ourselves were incapable of failure. Neither is there room for any moral adjustment that has to be made so that we do not forget our liability to failure. A confession of faith, which is an increase, by us, of our aliveness to our human nature in direct response to a perceived (by us) ignorance of human nature in others is in itself a thoroughgoing ethical act. It is also particular. No two such acts are the same, as it they were performed in line with, or on the basis of, some moral standard or principle. It is therefore impossible for such acts to be inappropriate. We cannot even imagine them out of the context of each singular aggravation and response.

Note that any comparative ignorance of human nature in others is not a stimulus to the peaceful and mature human being but an aggravation. It is a burden to us and it adds to our burden. Of course we tend to react, blindly; to resist any additional burden, just as we always incline to shrug off our own burden. That is the mechanism, which is really too predictable to be interesting. What does interest us no end is the extend to which we can actually choose to respond creatively to such aggravations. It does us immense good to do so and if it does no good to others it is certainly not our fault.

What we undertake to respond to, in terms of this social act, is not any shortfall we perceive in someone else but rather a given burden of aggravation in ourselves. Of course we cannot blind ourselves to the fact that such aggravations are due to the existential condition of someone other than ourselves and it does no harm for us to understand all such conditions in terms of ignorance and betrayal of human nature but it remains absolutely crucial that we learn and continue to differentiate between any aggravating increase of a burden on ourselves, to which we should wish to respond, ethically, and any resistant criticism, judgement or condemnation of the other one, which would after all testify to a lack of understanding on our part.

When I suggest that we understand the existential condition – let us say: the grief – of the other one, I agree that this is impossible unless we keep in mind that at any time we ourselves may stand in need of such understanding from someone whose faithful human nature is greater than ours. Any social action is therefore essentially humble.

*

54

When we think directly about society now and ask: "What is society?" we realize that so far we haven't a single image to go on. However we would like to be able to imagine a great number of social processes because that is how we have been schooled over the past two centuries, since sociologists first came on the scene to develop an image of society as an organization of psychic phenomena and picturable mechanisms that can be explained, in the sense of explained away, and predicted, in the sense of becoming controllable.

The modern mind, of course, does not distinguish between Society and society. Neither does it envision a great difference between community and society. Such distinctions only become relevant once popularity is isolated from humanity. A contemporary soul cannot do otherwise. I say soul rather than mind because for a contemporary human being mind and body are of equal importance as the two aspects of every soul, so that thinking and feeling go hand in hand.

Every contemporary soul seeks other contemporary souls and is glad to accept the difficulties along the way. Every genuine person is eager to communicate with other genuine persons and is willing to take pains to arrive at that goal. Every human being, male or female, has what it takes to sustain community and to overcome challenges to community.

We live in environments that are open to interpretation. A cultural environment is interpreted for us. If we ignore that fact we have a hard time finding our way through to a recognition of who we are, what we amount to and why we are here. We crave this recognition and try to achieve it by hook or by crook. Even our misguided Social achievements testify to that craving, to that knowledge of who, what and why we are. It is not something we can turn off but it can be aborted, become twisted and entirely misdirected. Finally, if we do not take matters into our own hands, we gain no satisfaction.

This is why all images of society as of a cultural environment may have historic relevance—may be interesting and entertaining—but cannot serve as moral justification or ethical guideline. In that sense society is always old. If instead of old images and illusions we want new and true realities we have to start thinking in terms of 'expressions of peace,' 'confessions of faith' and the like, as described on the previous pages. It means we are no longer enthralled by magical concepts of what might be if things were otherwise but we are at liberty to create the environment we need and want.

*

55

It becomes an embarrassment, even for those who are born with at least one foot in the human camp, to grow up in the company of male and female individuals whose greatest ambition is to edge one another out of the picture. This gives an impression of society as essentially selfish, in the sense that survival of the self or ego is invariably top of the agenda. A peculiar governance overshadows the creative mind and wears down the innocent affections. Those who carry within them the germ of an idea are force-fed trivial information and exposed to mechanistic education practices. Instinct, for example, can barely survive except in harness as mighty support.

Might has long been the god of the social environment. Anyone who thinks otherwise is faced with unpleasant consequences. The reason why might is so impressive rather than ridiculous is also the reason why society is viewed as an environment, as something one lives in and builds. We are often enough told we are responsible for the society we 'live in'. It's an extraordinary concept and highly questionable. All the images and concepts that decorate this environment, this idea of society as an environment, stem from the one source only, which is our illimitable desire to be duped. We walk around with this longing to have the world served up to us on a platter and any effort which promises as much is certified and supported.

The world worth inhabiting is not, however, interpreted or explained. It impresses us in ways that are wholesome for us to acknowledge. Especially our human environment is such that we really cannot be bothered with anyone's explanation of it while we search in ourselves for apposite replies and responses. If a stranger comes for a visit, I am not going to tell him the same old stories but I want to know what he has to say for himself. Society as those old familiar surroundings is forever ripe for our contempt and if we have vitality we will look elsewhere for the joy of being alive.

A critique of the social environment leaves it struggling for air. On one side we have the dominating factor which I would call the likelihood of everything that happens. An unlikely event must be dressed up before it can be credited. People develop an amazing facility for shutting out unlikely events. Interpretation has to make the advance of time acceptable just as explanation must precede any experience before it can be countenanced. These are the twin knee-jerk reactions to everything that is, so that it might appear to have been or to become. Now and again someone is born 'handicapped' in the sense that such reactions are foreign to him. What happens then is anybody's guess.

At the best of times the inhabitants of a cultural environment seek one another's society. This is the way of putting it when agreement is sought on the violability of human nature and when consensus is aimed at over the justifiability of the knee-jerk reaction. We have that on the other side. On one side the likelihood of all that happens and on the other side consensus on the need for immediate explanation and interpretation.

All would be fine if the explanation were not a case of explaining away and if the interpretation were not also a falsification. And of course the odd thing that happens is bound to fit in with our way of going but the important issues are the ones that surprise us because world is in truth ever new.

*

56

Civilized society is another case in point. Our cities are grand fortresses that will eventually be undermined from within. Our reasons for building them have always been defensive. The enemy is time. While human nature is eternally circumscribed, being open to influences that last forever, every effort we make to erect or institute mighty works results in something like a cry for help from our human nature which is not and cannot be mighty. Where society is a struggle in the shadow of mighty works the members of that society gradually become denatured and on meeting them it is as if one were trying to communicate with stones, except that even stones have a language.

Strength is something else altogether. Ask yourself, would you rather be strong or mighty? Might has an empty ring and makes a hollow sound. It requires posturing to assert itself. Its evidence has to precede it. There have to be those who attest to it before it can be sure of itself. Strength by comparison rests quietly in itself. It makes no demands.

Society as we imagine it has to be run and serviced like a machine. People are cogs. Let us increase the population for the sake of the economy. Give self-interest its head so that wealth shall be created. Can anyone imagine what this means: the happiness of the greatest number?

The social fallacy is to suppose that society can be directly influenced. How can you make a man happy by changing his surroundings? Indeed, how can you make a man happy? Why would you want to? So that he keeps out of your way? True enough, once I have made myself into a mighty guardian of society, happy men are less bother. A squirt of oil here, a switch replaced there, meanwhile I sit back; you will notice that contented grin.

Society as conditions, as surroundings – as environment. Society as the state – or as the State. Others will have to maintain it for us. Why not make the government responsible? We vote them into power and what thanks do we get? Sometimes they scramble to get into power, even though everyone knows that power allegedly corrupts. But corruption is not so bad. It reminds us we are creatures of the flesh – and so the argument goes. Neither rhyme nor reason is demanded, only impressive appearances.

A small matter of semantics should perhaps be attended to. Political power is a contradiction in terms. There can only

91

be political might, because might depends on conditions while power stems from ability. A strong man is able. He has the power to do good. Mischief is never a result of strength or power. 'Political might' makes more sense. It's what I would like and I might get away with it but it all depends on conditions being right. So we shape the electorate. Propaganda fashions the market for our ware. Opinion polls test the climate, that sort of thing. It is might that corrupts, not power. Then again it makes even more sense to say that might is a sign of corruption.

The same goes for the so-called 'will to power'. In our right mind we naturally want to do good and power implies the possibility and likelihood of achievement. But what I want is not necessarily what I will. As soon as force comes into it my so-called willing is spoiled. Might and force cohabit. Corruption and spoiling coincide. Check up on the society you 'live in', for its might and force content. Ask those who resist might and resent force why they do it and what they hope to gain by it.

*

57

How is it, anyway, that we become forceful? We develop a taste, an appetite for forceful action and behaviour. Does it always begin in us as a resistance to force, which resistance is bound to be just as forceful? We want to be free and we abhor constraint, that goes without saying but we also have a hankering for liberty, inasmuch as we would like to rid ourselves of all constraint and of anything that hampers our sense of well-being. As we know by now, freedom is not gained by diminishing constraints to liberty but by way of creative action and passion. A sense of well-being can therefore mean that we are about to experience constraint or that we creatively have something to offer. It's entirely up to us to decide which of the two is the case.

Everything related to force diminishes our sense of well-being. The force of circumstances, of other people's expectations, of obligations we assume, of compulsions and obsessions we experience, these we have to recognize for what they are before we can stop resisting them inasmuch as we resist them automatically. An experience of being forced is at the same time an act of forceful resistance, except that this act is not necessarily conscious. When we feel we are being forced we are also forcing, though not necessarily with a will. Any will to force would then be a case of our continuing to force but consciously and intentionally. The decision not to force would have to be understood as a decision to do something else rather than being forceful or forcing. This is important because all too often we suppose we make amends of sorts when we are just being forceful in some different way.

The solution is being merciful. As soon as we are merciful we are forceful no longer, neither intentionally nor accidentally.

Mercy is a creative response to forceful being and doing and to any perceived diminishment of our sense of well-being.

Mercy is also a valuable substitute for justice. It is only just that we should counter force with force, constraint with constraint. When we take recourse to the law and to legal proceedings, that is what we do. We do that consciously but perhaps not in the fullest awareness of what might be even better.

A merciful response to injustice is 'worth its weight in gold'. Injustice of course can take a myriad forms. If we think of a human being as a whole being, then any departure from wholeness can be seen as an injustice, in the sense of 'a lack of fit'. We cannot be responsible for being whole but only for meeting all preconditions. That famous sense of well-being is a sign that all preconditions have been met and that we are being mercifully influenced to become and be whole. If justice were invariably to be our portion we would never be healed or whole because we can at most manage an approximation, the rest being up to life itself, which is to say merciful good spirit. But while we ourselves insist on justice we cannot be mercifully influenced and therefore will not be whole.

Our insistence on justice is therefore every time a case of our selling ourselves short. By being merciful to others we open ourselves to the influence of merciful good spirit and as we know, this spirit is always present, whether we know it or not. Thinking and feeling mercifully is more than half the battle.

Justice can always be boiled down to this matter of 'an eye for an eye and a tooth for a tooth'. If we refine this a little and modernize it, it comes out as: 'I want my reward to reflect what I am worth. I don't want to be short-changed. I have an eye on the measure of my deserts and the two have to match. Every once in a while we recognize that this does not achieve wholeness for us, so most of the time we settle for an approximation.

The only way we can be sure we are the full measure is if our cup runs over. Once again, we cannot engineer that ourselves. We cannot make ourselves whole. We go in for self-sacrifice, and that is an ill-fated attempt to do just that. Sacrifice as such was probably invented as a means of disabusing oneself of the notion that one might be whole independently from the god one believed in. The first-born was sacrificed, or the best of the litter. One sacrificed to the gods so as to understand them, in the sense of standing under them.

One had experienced this situation of being bigger than one's boots. When this turned into a case of placating God, of bribing Him, He said: "The smoke from your sacrifice stinks in my nostrils". Small wonder. It would stink in ours too.

Today we know that sacrifice is a misguided attempt to achieve what has to come about as a response in its own good time to our merciful being and doing. Self-sacrifice is the modern version of sacrifice. The ancient version is the one described above. Self-sacrifice is at one and the same time, of course, an attempt to burn out or drown the ego and a willingness to *achieve* wholeness and/or holiness. First one has to mistake one's self for oneself and then one has to assume that god, or merciful good spirit, can be caused or brought about or bribed in some way. Many of us would sometimes like to believe that self-sacrifice will deliver the goods so we admire and praise one another for self-sacrificial action or behaviour. If we knew more about it at such times we would equate it with bribery and self-abuse. After all I've done for you, you still don't love me! Look, I have harmed myself for your sake, are you sure you don't want to love me?

I have mentioned these two errors: mistaking one's self for oneself and supposing one can force god's hand. There is a third one: Imagining we want to be loved when we actually only want to be liked. It means that secretly we don't really so much want to be whole as in the company of others who are as partial as we are. If enough of us get together who like one another we get a substitute sense of well-being and of wholeness and that is really then the society we would prefer and the society we suppose we would be happy with. The creative act of mercy is ruled out from the start. There is apparently no need for it.

Society as an environment, or a society as our environment, is imagined by us as a source and guarantee of whole-

95

ness. We labour under that misapprehension only until we understand that such a merciless environment can only deliver a feeble and short-lived substitute. The love we need is the influence that knows better than we do. Merciful love is tailored for those who are less than whole. We cannot make ourselves whole but we can be merciful. The merciful good spirit of love finds that irresistible, if I may put it that way. Our insistence on justice, on the other hand, closes the door to that spirit. A just society is based on the illusion that we can be whole among those who are like us, who like us and whom we like.

*

58

Society as environment really has nothing much going for it, in my opinion, except the benefit of a position where we may pause on our way and take a momentary breather. Surely no one in his right mind would wish to do more than pause—would wish, for example, to invest in some aspect of it, hoping for a return, or, for another example, to seek sympathy and comfort in that environment.

So we cannot say that this social environment ought to be a matter of indifference to us, any more than lampposts in the dark or cracks in the paving. If ever there was a need to tip our hat to simple facts, even mere facts, this is one. We ought to feel perfectly free to append labels: social milieu, social context, social conventions, social conscience, on and on, so that we may prefix an entire world, our own among a multiplicity of worlds, a thousand and one times with 'social' – without feeling that thereby we commit ourselves or do ourselves the least bit of good except maybe inasmuch as this helps us to keep our eyes open for what is real, natural and true, and beautiful and noble – and so on.

Always and again we will be cured of any social commitment or ease by the need to be merciful in the interest of being whole, being hale and hearty – being holy in the down to earth sense of that word. (The social holiness nowadays depends, I believe, on at least one miracle before official certification and this is only just.)

Every rigorous critique of society as an environment, as a popular, cultural, political etc. environment eventually must come to a halt in the face of what, within that context, is well-meaning and well-meant. I do not say well-intentioned but merely well-meant. I use the hyphen advisedly. What we 'mean' in such a case, being socially inclined, is after all well-being and no one has the right to tell us that we are not doing the best we can at that moment. The one who condemns us should first ask himself, has he something better to offer; the woods are full of those who can see through our foibles and they see nothing else.

What he does have a right, a duty, to tell us is how much more successful we would be in achieving what we mean if, after we have paused and taken a breather to be sure, we view all these social entities as pieces in a game, in a jigsaw puzzle, and then pass on – to something else, to something not social but perhaps to a gentle examination of what it really and truly is that we mean well. Evidently it has a character all its own and we do well not to shy away from that possibility. The use of the word 'mean' for 'intend' is interesting in this respect. Actually when I mean well I am only halfway to intending well but at least I am halfway there. So perhaps we should welcome in anyone the very physiology of 'meaning well', albeit not until we have created a bit of space between that and the social 'well-meaning', which attaches, after all, to some social end and to that extent is insupportable.

Even the most radical critique, therefore – this is what I mean – will acknowledge an initial desire for well-being, for true well-being, in the one who has been socio-environmentally side-tracked. On that the author of the critique builds his hope. It is the hope that fuels his intervention and the intervention is merciful. It is a merciful act. The intention is to show how we may prepare most practically for well-being and also to show by example that it does on occasion come about – but that it cannot be made to happen. The last part is of the least importance to the merciful practitioner. Of primary importance for him is that he demonstrates communality in comparison to sociability, and community as environment in comparison to society as environment.

*

59

We mean well, we social beings, inasmuch as we flex the bow and release the sinew but 'arrow', the very word, escapes us – unless it sticks in our craw. The mark is never hit; it is not even missed. That makes it hard for us to improve our aim.

However we go through this exercise because somehow it seems right. Better, it seems better. Who would not wish to be better, at least to seem better? The social environment in which we would be ready, if not eager, to lose ourselves—to lose our name, our identity—is one where everything is better and is done better. There is always room for improvement, we say. On such friendly terms we encourage one another. Be silent for a moment, while one passes who actually does things well, for he is not one of us. Now let us get back to the many interesting and exciting ways of flexing this bow.

The one who passes notices the silence and is riven by contempt. He prefers to be well and to do things well and the better-doers and better-knowers set off in him a nausea – which puzzles him. He would like to be able to view them from unaffected distances, the way he strolls past less than mediocre paintings in a gallery. Smile knowingly and pass on.

But that knowing smile would be a better-knowing smile and that frightens him. All else being equal, there is a world of difference between stepping in, open eyed, and being sucked in, blindly. That is the 'choice'. Perfect indifference is the ideal he rejects, because it is an ideal and because he acknowledges wryly from experience that if he did not reject it, it would reject him. Sometimes, from sheer cheek, he likes to have that confirmed. He wants it in writing. Ink or pencil will do.

Once we know how to be and do well, there is no going back – to being and knowing better. The comparative rug has been pulled out from under our feet. The common denominator has become uncommon. The better-knower has many choices. He can even manage his type of indifference, such as when he looks away, clings to his kind and remains silent for the interim. However the one who knows how to be and do well is perfectly free to be and do so and therefore he has no choices at all. Prison, in comparison, is no choice but an accident.

So here he is, the well-doer, riven by contempt. The accident was, perhaps, unavoidable. He is no longer well. His well has momentarily dried up. Or has something poisoned it? Shall he waste time to figure that out? Shall he scrutinize his present environment to identify the culprit? Presently, let us hope 'momentarily', his environment is social. He has become infected, no arguing with that. His contempt tempts him no end. How he despises those well-meaning better-knowers without arrows – apparently without conscience or memory of arrows! He himself has now become arrow-minded. How he would like to let fly! He can see them banding together at his approach.

All this time he is becoming more false to himself. He also misjudges his environment. He judges it, therefore he misjudges it. He knows only the one god, so is it any wonder that he feels momentarily forsaken? These others worship a multitude.

Suddenly it is given to him to remember what it is he can do – who he can be – when it appears to him that his well has run dry or been poisoned. Since he cannot be well he can certainly be – himself. Since he cannot do well he can surely do – somehow. In short, he gives birth to an artwork.

Oh blessed mystery! – to give birth to a work! He utters the lyric plaint. He states the epic case. He allows himself the tragicomic gesture. Perhaps he only comes up with a quote from some cosmic codex, to tide himself over and that's all it takes. In short, he helps himself out with contemporary art.

In a fascinating sense he relies on the future to bring him into the here and now where he is conjoined with the past. "The times were out of joint, oh cursed spite" but he knows that "his name is written on high" and that the future is "the coming One", not the arrowless multitude, sectarian to the core. All this help he gets as he 'gives birth to an artwork'. Numerous nurses surround him and one special midwife takes care.

*

60

The role of art in society has fascinated some of the best minds and hearts over the years and centuries. If we inquire into the circumstances under which a significant art work comes to fruition we find ourselves within a context not much different from the one that has bearing on why an art work should be significant in the first place.

Our critique of society as environment has left us with an image of it as largely self-contained and misguided. Needless to say such a critique could not take advantage of the previously worked out distinction of Society from society, where the former has never really existed except as a risk and temptation, while the latter always exists in reality but as secondary and coincidental to the search for community. The critique of society as environment must therefore be seen, both as to intention and conclusion, as a clearing of the ground for society as possible transition on the way to community, which implies its function, by the way, as a sustainable buffer zone in the face of anti-communal elements. All intentionally social 'impulses' are anti-communal by definition and one can certainly both imagine and actually see evidence of an art that is Social inasmuch as it excludes creativity and concentrates on mass culture. But such art precisely is not significant inasmuch as it does not point beyond our likes and dislikes. If for a moment we were to imagine ourselves as social beings we would soon enough understand how our urge to impress one another under those circumstances would be uppermost and we would not see any reason why such impressive effects and executions should not be called art, as long as practical usefulness were excluded.

Indeed it should be called Art, in correspondence to Society. The magical elements would be pre-eminent here too and any so called work of art would rise higher in our estimation to the degree that it shocked or shamed or stunned. Those are the three impressions that predominate in Social Art and they are mighty effects and would therefore appeal to our secret admiration for forces and mechanisms.

101

We never have to look far for Social art because it crowds the public domain. It competes for prizes and solicits reward on the market place. Social Art objects are hawked to the highest bidder and the magic that clings to them determines their worth for those who acquire them. This is not to say that an outlandish price tag on a painting defines it as <u>A</u>rt but it does mean that it is being treated as though it were Art even though it was created, and perhaps for a legitimate purpose, such as a genuinely <u>s</u>ocial invitation to feeling and thought.

So just as the social impulse is ultimately divisive in that it prevents any communal achievement, so must the art which springs from such a non-creative impulse be ultimately destructive. An at times quite innocent appearance belies an underlying seductiveness in favour of the popular myths and therefore at the expense of human nature and abusive of reality.

*

61

It might be an interesting question to ask why a Social being should welcome being shocked, shamed or stunned by artificial experience. What we might do well to keep in mind in this connection is our collective weakness for mass, myths and magic. I call it a collective weakness because the club, the group and the crowd bring it out. As members of a clan, clique or tribe we are singularly exposed to certain real dangers which threaten what we perceive to be the benefits of such sodality. These dangers can be summed up as loss of individuality, as loss of identity and integrity. While we remain unwilling to relinquish our Social status we try to limit the dangers as we cling to the perceived benefits. The artificial shock and shame are to recall us to our individuality. However a thousand and one things are wrong with this. Since our Socialized individuality is tied up and tangled in a spider's web of bad commitments, any protection of it against risk is really pointless. Just as the Art is insignificant because it does not point beyond concerns of self-interest, so are the artificial effects of shock and shame not to the point. All the same one can understand the theory behind this strategy. The mechanics are transparent. An individuality that is short-circuited and not allowed to develop into personhood becomes rigid and a set psyche comes into being. We become fearfully certain of our self in our stiff-necked way and the shock is to break that certainty, to confuse our obsessional stare at the world. The shame is supposed to address the moral issue. Loss of identity and integrity is experienced as guilt and the artificial shame is to redress the balance by facilitating a purity of heart. However what use are a flexible neck and an innocent heart if once again we seek recourse to our ego?

*

62

Our weakens for mass, myths and magic can be identified. I can identify these weaknesses for collectivity and for a relinquishment of my individuality in myself. I may acknowledge these collective weaknesses. Such acknowledgement is at the same time a desire for strength. No one admits to a weakness unless he has some notion, however instinctive or intuitive, of an equal and opposite strength.

Let's describe some aspects of these weaknesses.

We imagine that if we are <u>massive</u> we will not be held responsible or accountable. We give ourselves over as raw material, to be handled and made into something, into whatever. We no longer have to think, our minds are made up for us, our hearts are stilled. This appeals to us especially when we grow weary, due to pain or a repeated frustration of our efforts. We have perhaps tried to 'make' but have messed up so often that now let someone or something 'make' <u>us</u>. We take a fancy to a dictator. Ah, to be putty in someone's hands! We join a cult and let the leader tell us how to be. The challenge of personality no longer bothers us because we now have a mass identity, which is in fact more like a label. Giving in to this weakness is catastrophic because our human nature becomes less and less accessible as we have one breakdown of our individuality after the other. We experience such breakdowns as acquisitions of beliefs and credentials, as increases of conviction and certainty. If we have any real friends they might speak of these in terms of brainwashing, hysteria, mass hypnosis and the like.

It is of course not true that everyone has his own unique and individual tendency to be weak, since the weakness is defined precisely as a loss of individuality and uniqueness. It might help us to speak of mass, myth and magic as three <u>types</u> of weakness and an individual might incline more to one than to the other but this only labels him, as a Kenilworth football club supporter or as a Christian Scientologist and has nothing to do with individuality or personality. It makes him typical, not unique.

If I proudly declare myself as a member of some faction, this does not mean that I have acknowledged a weakness and am therefore on the road to strength. On the other hand it's no use my trying to combat this particular self-indulgence, because that would only throw me into some other camp. The only thing that can help me is if, in recognition of present circumstances, I acknowledge my weakness, perhaps even my typical weakness, with the understanding that I should prefer strength instead.

Before we take a look at the other two types of weakness, for myths and magic, let's recognize that any acknowledgement of such weakness is creative. This insight has led a representative German author to speak of his entire opus as: "...eine große Konfession", which means something like 'a great confession or acknowledgement'. We need to be aware of this creativity inasmuch as it forms the basis of specific art, which is to say social art.

We could go on to identify three species of art in view of the type of weakness that is more emphatically acknowledged. This would not involve classification or categories. It is more like an intuitive feel we can acquire for making optimum use of creative art examples and products.

We are creative from the beginning of our acknowledgement of our typical weakness right up to the point where we deal artfully with specific issues in the light of day. However we are not artfully creative until we have come out of ourselves, having dealt with our inward weakness, and have begun applying ourselves in a specific way to some particular manifestation of weakness.

It must seem odd, boiling creativity down like this to weakness and strength, to an overcoming of weakness and a gaining of strength. Strength, however, is fundamental to our readiness and preparedness for life. It would be foolish to suppose that a weak beings can live. It is precisely by way of our manifest weaknesses that we unconsciously signal to one another our need for help. The basic constituent of that help is strength. How we render and supply that help, that is our art.

We artfully share the strength we ourselves have gained creatively. All art is creative but not all creativity is artful. Only outward creativity is artful.

*

63

We may call it social art if it stems from an overcoming in ourselves, by ourselves, of such a weakness, of such self-indulgence in, for instance, a mass identity. There may not after all be much point in distinguishing between different species of social art in view of which a particular weakness is perhaps more emphatically being overcome. Using the word specific to describe social art should however be helpful because it indicates the way such skills are directed by us, as appropriately as possible, towards areas of perceived need. Anything we do skilfully to help others conquer this weakness in themselves is artful in this sense. So I may have such a purpose in mind when I speak to you or do something for you, arranging some matter in a way calculated to let you perhaps see how much better off you might be if you sought strength instead of abiding in weakness. Again it would be in no one's interest if I criticized your weakness. It would certainly not be artful or creative. In the important sense I want to share with you my pleasure in strength, the pleasure I take in being strong rather than weak, strong rather than forceful or mighty. This urge to share my pleasure would be automatically triggered off in me by my sensitivity to your weakness, so it would not be a case of my intellectually pinpointing your weakness and then deciding to help you over it. This is important to keep in mind, so that I identify correctly in myself this pleasant urge, this urgent pleasure, as the art impulse that it is. I might mistake it and waste it.

If I do want to criticize, judge or condemn, I am on a totally different wavelength and need to be reminded as soon as possible of my lack of creativity. Perhaps someone near to me will be sensitive to my weakness and ... But this bring us around to that second weakness which I called a weakness for myths.

What is it about myths that attracts us?

In a nutshell, they are pretensions of our psyche to completeness and wholeness.

Quickly let me review what I mean by psyche. Our soul, our divine being which we have on account of our human natural faith and which we do not have in the absence of such faith, is not sensible to us, we have no sense experience of it until it is at risk of being abused or neglected, and then we have the inward experience of our psyche. Elsewhere I have called the psyche the shadow of our soul. We cannot be in the possession of 'our' psyche as we can be, in patience, in possession of our soul but we are more or less obsessed or even possessed by it. We are in high or low spirits, in delirium, in hysteria, in a mood. We are frantic, obsessive, giddy, melancholy or in despair. All these are psychic states and therefore signals of a need for a change which we can bring about. A psyche is evidence of a soul, but of a soul at risk.

That would be a quick way of coming to grips with this complex issue. It is complicated only because conventionally no difference is made between psyche and soul. What matters for us here at the moment is that psychic states, or a psyche at all (actually there are only psychic states) cannot be anything in itself. We do well therefore not to settle at the foot of the signpost but to take the path it indicates.

What we all too often do instead in our weakness is look for excuses that will allow us to give those states an appearance of permanence. At first we try to prolong the pleasant states, the high spirits, the excitement, the energetic feeling, and when that falls through we take a perverse pleasure in prolonging the unpleasant ones, because, as we suppose, even an unpleasant psyche is better than none.

Myths are our means for prolonging and hopefully making permanent our psychic states. We hope that with the help of them we can make psyche do duty as our soul. We try to achieve a soul by way of accrediting myths but this is always a kind of mischief. Mercifully we are never allowed to succeed in this because it would render us 'truly monstrous'.

I am not going to point at any particular myths, although there is no lack of them, but it gives me pleasure to share with you the strength I get from doing without them – to the extent that I actually do without them.

*

64

The myth-making faculty can spring into action in anyone. We are all potential liars, if not on one level of consciousness then on another. Again, it is much safer to acknowledge this than to deny it.

This tendency to myth-making is our willingness to make psychic states do. We suppose ourselves innocent if we make them do. In comparison to soul however and, so to speak, against the backdrop of our soul, psychic states are seen clearly. They reveal something. What they reveal, generally, is shortfall and neglect. We fail to rise to occasions and we miss opportunities. This, however, can only make sense in view of an overall goal or achievement. Where nothing is undertaken there can be no failure.

Our overall goal is true and real human being. It is to be whole as persons in community. It is to be mature and capable of nurturing to maturity. It is to have life and to have it in abundance. It is to be creatively skilful, to know what it means to do good and to be helpful, to be ethically active and aware.

We are at liberty to aim at this goal or not but we are not free to do so. Unless we aim at this goal we are not free. We are merely at liberty. Freedom comes along with proximity to achievement of that end.

If, instead of aiming at this goal, we pursue psychic states as ends in themselves, we go against our own safe and sound human nature. We are not true to ourselves.

There can be only two or three reasons for doing this. One is total ignorance of the possibility of such a goal. Another is the shame and guilt that reflects on us whenever we become aware of our psychic states, in comparison to soul, as neglect and shortfall. No one likes to be ashamed or guilty. Even less do we like to <u>feel</u> ashamed or guilty. What do we do? We get rid of whatever makes us feel that way. If we don't feel guilty we must be innocent. If we don't feel ashamed we must be chaste.

However, not so. For periods of time it is possible to be guilty and shameful without feeling it and without being conscious of it. Myths help us to prolong those periods. We make and adopt myths for that purpose. Then we need to be reminded of this falsehood. The reminder causes us to feel horror and terror. We do experience horror and terror not only because our guilt and shame is once again brought to our attention but also because we cannot help but notice that our myths are false and therefore untenable.

*

65

If our eye is generally on the goal, then guilt and shame can be welcome to us as to how we can make our aim more accurate. At first, of course, we always shrink from guilt and shame but this shrinking is itself a part of the guilt and shame, so if we can deal properly with the shrinking we are

109

on our way to recuperation. If we do not deal with it, the shrinking becomes a shirking – of our duty to become whole.

How can we deal with this guilty and shameful shrinking as soon as we experience it? Simply by calling to mind what we know of our soul, of our psychic states in comparison to it, of our life goal, and so on. It's obviously important to learn as much as possible about this. In this way too we acknowledge it.

It might help if we work out for ourselves an image of our soul (not a picture) because that makes it more memorable. When we feel guilt or shame we want to be able to act fast. So we might imagine our soul as that which both urges and leads us on to our goal and that of which we are in possession when we are most nearly on course to our goal. We might think of it as a working principle or a lively operation. It is definitely not a feeling or a state. These pertain to our psyche, which is fragmentary, uncentred and unpredictable. Our soul is reliable, central and whole. It holds everything else in place and makes the details of our existence meaningful.

A scoundrel feels neither guilt nor shame because he has no good goal and his soul is not accessible to him. A fool feels neither guilt nor shame because he says there is no such thing as a soul.

Our denial of guilt and shame can become almost automatic. We might call it the bad habit per se. We react with a myth so fast that we barely notice ourselves doing it. The myth ends up being something neither inward nor outward, where we operate creatively and with skill, but inside or outside us, where we are helpless.

It would be quite wrong therefore to say that myths are created. Creativity always implies an overcoming, a transcending, a seeing through or an understanding. Myths are

110

precisely results of an unwillingness to do this. Technically we should not even say they are made because they more or less happen, with a degree of connivance or collusion by us. (We co-operate with our soul, we collude with psyche.)

Why do I call them myths? Because they are essentially reactions to mythic influence. They are our rejections of that influence.

Due to mythic influence we are completed, perfected, made whole. We are always and forever influenced mythically. We have been told about that and we either believe it and become whole or we do not believe it and become fragmentary, incomplete, torn between alternatives and such like. If we do not search for the truth we lie. If we do not accept in our hearts what we are told, that the goal of our life is sanctioned by this influence, then it is not sanctioned. The power of believing is as instrumental in the end as our faith is fundamental in the beginning. All our achievements must in the end be crowned by this mythic influence, as by the spirit of truth. The good goals we set ourselves must include an ultimate openness and receptivity to completion and perfection from without or from within.

It would not be wrong but perhaps helpful to speak of mythic influence of the spirit of truth. Myths are denials of mythic influence just as falsehoods are rejections of the truth. When we speak of that which is mythic we refer to the truth inasmuch as it is told. Is it conceivable that someone has been around somewhere for a number of years and never been told the truth? Is that still possible today?

So the myths with which we unfortunately protect ourselves at times against the challenge of a soul which might be ours are also language based and word centred, but reactively so. They are typical myths when we tell tales to cover up our culpability. Or we gather information in such a way that our

111

faith is blinded or so that our faculty of belief becomes irrelevant. What we end up with then is a myth, or several myths. Our social environment offers an endless collection of myths. Some of these are drummed into us when we are children. Others are collectively sustained so that we may have something on hand when we need a quick explanation for why we follow the popular lead or a ready justification for having prompted bad behaviour or having blocked some good deed. Especially in a modern culture one is never short of all sorts of dubious reasons for stopping halfway in pursuit of some truly ethical goal and turning back, faithful no longer to one's human nature but to convention and convenience.

The good news is that this weakness of ours can be just as creatively overcome as our weakness for mass. Let us love the truth and be receptive to mythic influence. Let us listen carefully to those who speak to us, both young and old, for the truth will out, either because of what they say or in spite of what they say, and what a pity if we miss it because we prefer our psychic state, our arrogance or our timidity, our happiness or our sadness, to the strength of wisdom and instruction!

We can see quite plainly how there is a need for our own acknowledgement of such weakness if we are to come up with an effective art skill in the end. And by art skill I mean every activity or passivity during which we exercise our personality, whatever the medium, whether language, gesture or clay and whatever the work or product. The only work greater than that stems from personhood, which is however communal and not social. In the present essay we look no further than to social manifestations of art skills.

*

66

Two of our weaknesses I have discussed so far. The weakness for mass, like the one for myths, must be acknowledged by us if we are to make a strengthening contribution by way of our society.

Society can no longer be an environment to us, something we long for or shun and experience as outside of us if not inside, once we have become personally active. It should be mentioned here that 'personalities' cannot be active like this, creatively based and skilfully artful. When we refer to someone as a personality we mean someone who has acquired status vis-à-vis society as an environment and we cannot really take someone like that seriously. Such status is ephemeral, is insubstantial, very much like the environment that individual has chosen to impress. Personalities, like celebrities, are media 'creations', except that precisely no creation is involved but a most unusual series of accidents that happen to Social beings in their social environment. Keep in mind that a social environment is itself at best impotent and effete.

A discussion of this series of accidents brings us round finally to our third weakness, the weakness for magic.

Imagine yourself craving the Social connection. You want to be popular, you want to be praised, you want to be liked. You expend a deal of energy performing tasks that will hopefully endear you to a public. You have taken your eye off any individually creative contribution you might make and your human nature as the origin and urgency of your individual personality no longer interests you because you have decided to guess what 'the people' want and to meet those wants. You sense in people the very weaknesses we have been discussing and it seems to you that you can indulge your own weaknesses if you pander to theirs.

Or conversely imagine that someone like that appeals to you somehow, by way of some skill he or she has developed. He panders to your weakness and you sense momentarily that here is your chance to indulge your weakness with pleasure and impunity.

In both cases something is liable to happen that is difficult if not impossible to quantify.

The first thing to consider here is that what is about to go on is diametrically opposed to any communal union that might be brought about. During such a communal union and in line with it, human nature would come to fruition. Two human natures would become one or even several human natures would become one, let us say, 'on a higher level'.

Where two or more individuals have lost interest in their human nature and have opted for popularity instead, the exact opposite happens. Instead of a union of beings there is a proliferation of things.

Also, the union of beings would be on a 'higher' plane, where higher means closer to good and it would to a certain extent be an achievement, a work, inwardly based, outwardly manifest. The get-together of the popular individuals, by comparison, facilitates the sinking to a lower plane, where lower means closer to bad and instead of power being exercised, forces are unleashed, accidentally;   mechanisms are exploited and might is tasted.

What the popular individuals crave initially has nothing to do with forces and mechanisms nor with things of any sort. They want to indulge their weaknesses, with pleasure and impunity. They have no doubt about the possible pleasure but the impunity is sometimes a bit of a problem.

None of the three weaknesses we have mentioned is ever experienced in isolation from the rest. The weakness for

114

magic, which is what we are focusing on now, cannot be understood separately from the weakness for mass and myths. However the main ingredient that typifies the leaning to magic is the individual's desire for the union he would be able to achieve personally if he were not addicted to popular pleasure. As he gravitates more and more towards this pleasure which he mistakes for the 'real thing', his human nature, however far he has neglected it, is bound to signify to him that neglect, to point out to him the results of his abuse. The proliferation of things, of mighty forces and mechanisms, is liable to come as a surprise to him. It is not what he expected and certainly not what he was after. Understanding is at an extreme minimum. No doubt he has had a taste of the illicit pleasure. This is not pleasure he has given but pleasure he has taken. However now that he knows this pleasure he has to protect both it and himself against these monstrosities that threaten. It turns into a trade-off. He will do his utmost to negate, defuse and harness the things that confront him but his reason for doing so is his supra-personal union.

I referred to the backlash to his mischief as a series of accidents. While he insists on being weak and on continuing to be weak his chief preoccupation will be an endless number of attempts at some predictability of these accidents. If only he can ban them into some sort of order he will be able to master them and enjoy his pleasure undisturbed.

Meanwhile his human nature is less and less his. He knows it less, he is less aware of it, little realizing that the urge for union is itself at its root human natural, that the things he has piled on him are really frustrated beings, that the forces are signs of abused power and that the mechanisms are "the tears of the ignored law", as someone has called them.

At the same time there is the massive avoidance of responsible and accountable individuality and also the projection of myths as protection against the mythic influence of true spirit. All three elements figure in this equation of weakness which accounts for society as an environment.

The combined danger is evident now. Human nature, which gives rise to individuality, is massively pushed away. The spirit of mythic truth can no longer influence because of falsehood as a barrier and the very goal of humanity, which is personal community in the light of day, is being magically supplanted.

*

67

Now as we know all too well from our own daily existence, an accident is not merely a chance happening, uncaused but rather a sign of neglect or abuse. We can read those signs intelligently and improve our performance in future.

The same goes for all those signs of neglect or abuse of our human nature, of the mythic spirit of truth and of our ethical purpose in life.

With regard to our sound and safe human nature, we may keep in mind that of itself it has what it takes to urge us on to some recognition of our individuality and if we accept responsibility and make ourselves accountable for that, we can be said to be true to our human nature. However in order to go on from there to personality we have to take account of and respond to what I usually call merciful good spirit of love. This spirit determines our nature in such a way that we cannot rest in our individual being.

When we contemplate our various weaknesses therefore and put ourselves to the task of gaining the strength that is proportionately ready for us, we have a threefold help on which we can rely. We have the dynamic of our human na-

116

ture, the sanction of true myth and the power of love. In reliance on all three we soon overcome the weaknesses that define our dependence on society as environment as we become personally active and artfully creative in terms of society as available transition to community.

Once again it might be wise to remind ourselves that what I have called specific social art is really any skill we use to let those around us know, if they wish to know, how strength is preferable to weakness. Our acknowledgement of our own inclination to such weakness will always be somehow fed into such skills, otherwise we fail hypocritically. The sheer luminosity of our personal example will sometimes suffice. Our interest will always have to include the ethical welfare of others. It's no use pretending that we can be socially creative in isolation. Any social commitment however must point beyond society. Those who are ignorant of community and personhood will always be weak and tempt to weakness to some extent. They will present social benefits as ends in themselves, thereby blinding others to the strength they might gain. Of course it is up to all of us in the end what use we make of whatever is available.

* * * * *

* * *

*

www.ingramcontent.com/pod-product-compliance
Lightning Source LLC
Chambersburg PA
CBHW060408290526
45791CB00002B/662